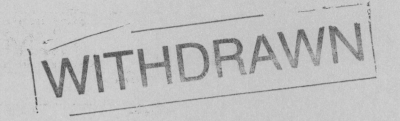

Advanced Textiles
for Health and Wellbeing

Advanced Textiles
for Health and Wellbeing

Marie O'Mahony

with 231 colour illustrations

Thames & Hudson

page 2: Composite, Design Composite
GmbH, Austria.

page 5: 3D nonwoven, Volz Luftfilter
GmbH, Germany.

First published in the United Kingdom
in 2011 by Thames & Hudson Ltd,
181A High Holborn, London WC1V 7QX

Designed by Bianca Wendt

British Library Cataloguing-in-
Publication Data
A catalogue record for this book is
available from the British Library

ISBN 978-0-500-51587-7

Printed and bound in China by Toppan
Printing

To find out about all our publications,
please visit **www.thamesandhudson.com**.
There you can subscribe to our
e-newsletter, browse or download our
current catalogue, and buy any titles that
are in print.

PAGE 8
INTRODUCTION

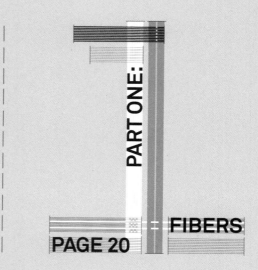

PART ONE:

PAGE 20   FIBERS

PART TWO:

PAGE 104
HABITAT

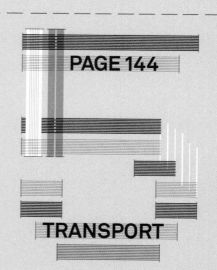

PAGE 144

TRANSPORT

PAGE 42

FABRIC
STRUCTURES

PAGE 80
SURFACE

PAGE 178

PERSONAL

PAGE 202
ENVIRONMENT

PAGE 234
GLOSSARY

PAGE 236
DIRECTORY OF SUPPLIERS

PAGE 238
BIBLIOGRAPHY

PAGE 239
PHOTO CREDITS

PAGE 240
INDEX

Spacewalk, NASA, USA, 2009.
The space industry has historically
been behind many of the new textile-
related technologies, particularly
those relating to applications in
health and safety. In-space applications
range from the spacesuit to thermal
blankets which protect the Hubble's
electronics as shown here.

'There is nothing closer to the big bang of design,
to its prime reason to exist, than objects that
deal with self-preservation', Paola Antonelli,
Safe: Design Takes on Risk, 2005

Avoiding death is the most fundamental human
instinct. The majority try to avoid physical injury
and fatality by taking active steps. However,
for those who are not faced with the imminent
possibility of death, it is not enough merely to be
alive. Quality of life has become the new alchemy.

The early alchemists sought the elusive philosopher's stone and were part of a long spiritual tradition looking for the secret to eternal life. Our present knowledge of the strength and frailties of the human body not only helps us to live longer, healthier lives, but also gives us a hyperawareness of our mortality. We use all the means at our disposal to prevent damage to our bodies and to care for them. This extends to all aspects of our lives, from how we live and eat to the products we choose to buy. This has led to a significant growth in the market area of advanced textiles as they form the basis for many of the most innovative emerging designs.

The World Islands, *Nakheel, United Arab Emirates*. This series of around 300 artificial islands has been shaped into the continents of the world. They include community islands, private homes, estate homes and resorts, including some luxury resorts. Geosynthetics have played a significant role in their development.

Venus Chair, *Tokujin Yoshioka Inc., Japan.* The exhibition installation of the designer's 'Venus' series of biotech gel chairs that have been grown from natural crystals on a textile scaffold.

Roadrunner, Bill Burns, USA.
Watercolours from artist Bill Burns'
'Safety Gear for Small Animals'
series which highlight the impact
of human action on wildlife. The
devices illustrated are human safety
gear that has been resized to fit
small animals.

While most fabrics can perform some protective or beneficial function, the focus of this book is to look at those that are specifically designed to contribute actively to our wellbeing. Part 1 looks at the materials themselves and Part 2 is given to the designs that utilize these materials.

The Fibers chapter shows how fibers are being formed in a great variety of ways using, for instance, techniques that allow synthetic fibers to be so highly engineered that they are finer than a human hair. It reveals how an unremarkable surface can house an intricate structure with a hollow centre that performs great feats of climate control or carries other benefits. 'Fabric structures' are building on the performance of these fibers, extending their capabilities through their construction. The range and indeed scale is breathtaking, from the tiniest medical stent invisible to the naked eye to large composites for the aerospace industry. 'Surfaces' such as embedding, coating and finishing add a further dimension to these materials and can also form the main function itself. Anti-microbial, anti-static, odour-absorbing and flame-retardant treatments are just some of those that are being used individually and increasingly in combination to provide multiples of performance. It seems the only limit to what is possible is the imagination of the textile and chemical engineer, who seem determined to prove that anything is possible.

Clothing is our most intimate daily contact with fabrics and it is here that we can find the widest range of applications. Garments that protect against chemical hazards, help keep us cool or

Ford Rouge Center, William McDonough + Partners, Dearborn, Michigan, 2003. The ten-acre living roof provides thermal and acoustic insulation for the workers and a home for wildlife as can be seen from the bird's eggs in the foreground.

eXasis, Rinspeed, Switzerland, 2007. Concept car from Frank M. Rinderknecht in a collaboration with Bayer MaterialScience AG to create a lightweight transparent body. The upholstery fabric is from Strähle + Hess and includes a Technogel cast textile for the arm and headrests.

warm, or help to build up our strength are all being developed and refined. Transportation sees textiles being used to provide acoustic and vibration control inside cars as well as providing lightweight and fuel-efficient composites for aeroplane wings or helicopter blades. Textiles have a long history of being used as habitats, with the traditional yurt now providing a blueprint for sustainable climate control. Buildings such as the Water Cube built in Beijing for the 2008 Olympic Games may look very different from a yurt, but they share a common desire

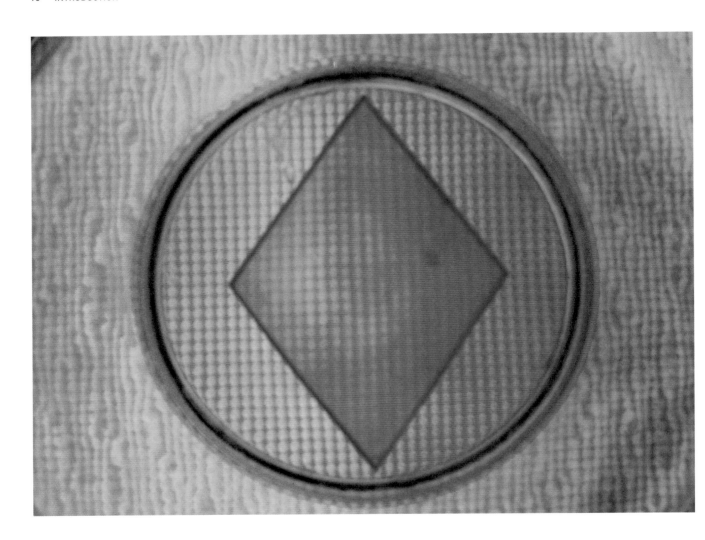

Harlequin Coat, Orlan, France,
2007. Detail of a biotechnological
coat produced at SymbioticA.
In the manner of a traditional
harlequin coat, elements have
been brought in from different
origins and include the artist's
own skin cells as well as those
of a black woman and a marsupial.

to achieve a comfortable temperature for their occupants in the most efficient way possible. The issue of sustainability runs throughout so that the Environment chapter considers how fabrics are being used in the urban and rural environment. We see them protect crops from the heat of the sun and landslide zones from further erosion. There are also examples of the development of living roofs that help to offset the environmental impact of our buildings. For each of these applications there are a number of innovative solutions, many of which combine design and engineering.

The coming together of the technical and the aesthetic is key to the emergence of this area of advanced textiles for wellbeing and health. For too long the two have remained separate in education, industry and the design and engineering studios. We are now seeing a shift in thinking to bring the two together so that materials that perform also look good and are pleasant to handle. One example is the fabric used for acoustic insulation in buildings. It has long been hidden behind cladding, performing but invisible to the occupants – a textile Quasimodo. Now we are seeing these materials used in full view, bringing form, texture and colour – all of which are now seen as being part of their function.

Disguise garment, *Eunjeong Jeon, Australia.* LED-illuminated garment which is designed to morph and change colour to help the wearer feel protected and safe. The main garment is made from engineered felted wool.

FIBERS

Developments in fiber and yarn technologies are having an impact on both natural and synthetic materials. Fiber engineers are creating fibers that combine the benefit of both, sometimes even bringing them together literally to form hybrids. Performance is enhanced by the handle and comfort associated with natural fibers, while natural fibers are engineered to be as easy to care for as artificial fibers. These synthetics and hybrids are far removed from the original 'artificial silk' rayon which in reality had nothing like the handle and lustre of the natural fiber it purported to re-create. While the original synthetics were poor imitations of more expensive natural materials, the engineered fibers that we are seeing today are much more highly valued in every sense.

One of the most significant changes to occur in the textile industry has been in attitude. Research and development laboratories no longer try to imitate nature; instead they look to combine the finest qualities of natural and man-made while seeking out their own aesthetics and benefits for the consumer. History has shown the wisdom in this: it was only when plastics stopped trying to pretend to be ivory or wood that designers, manufacturers and consumers began to value them for their own unique qualities. As new production techniques become available, the opportunities for engineering fibers and yarns stretch from large-scale to the nano, invisible to the naked eye.

Below: **Dyneema Chair,** *Studio Geenen, The Netherlands, 2009.* The elegant simplicity of this chair demonstrates the versatility of high-strength yarns. DSM's Dyneema has been used in a composite to create the structural elements, in a woven fabric where little flexibility is needed and as a knit for stretch on the seat and back.

Opposite: **Glass and carbon fibers,** *SILTEX Flecht- und Isoliertechnologie Holzmüller GmbH & Co. KG, Germany.* This braided structure shows two high-strength yarns combined. The glass fiber is white and the black yarn is carbon fiber.

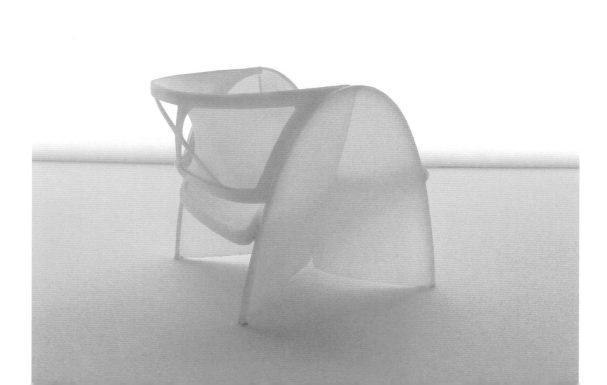

Opposite and below: **Glass and aramid fibers (opposite) and braided carbon and glass fibers (below),** *SILTEX Flecht- und Isoliertechnologie Holzmüller GmbH & Co. KG, Germany.* These braided, high-strength fibers are often identifiable by their colour – white denotes glass, black carbon and yellow aramid fibers. Advances in technology are now starting to allow these yarns to be coloured more.

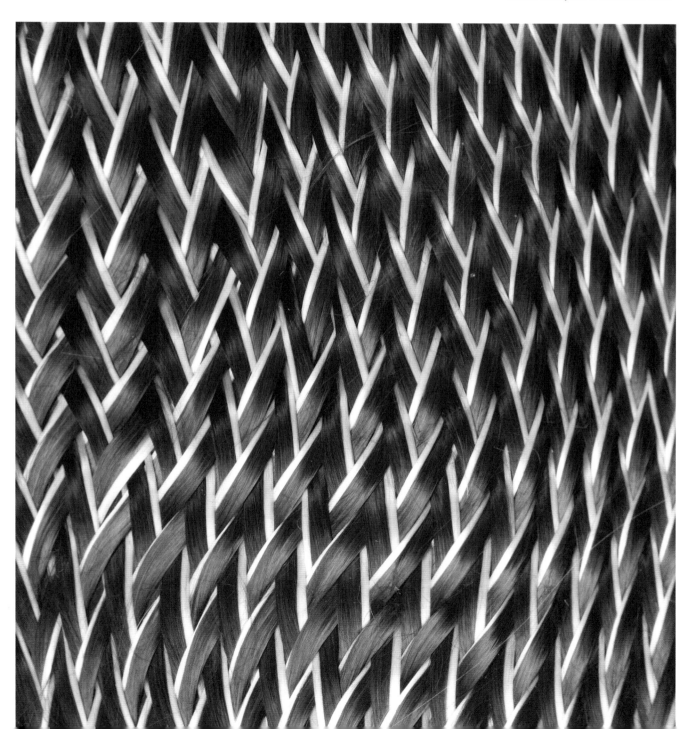

Recycled PET fibers,
Teijin Ltd, Japan. These Eco Circle wicking fabrics move perspiration to the surface of the fabric so it can evaporate and increase the comfort of the wearer. These fibers have been produced using the Eco Circle closed loop recycling system. The grey fabric contains 100% of the environmentally friendly yarn and the red includes almost 70%.

Climate change is forcing a dramatic change in all aspects of our lives and the textile industry is part of this process. The environmental impact of fabrics starts with their origin. The provenance of fibers and yarns has to be traceable and accountable in a universally recognizable manner. Oeko-Tex is respected worldwide for its accreditation process as it grants certification for fixed terms after which manufacturers must re-submit. This is changing the way in which both natural and synthetic materials are produced and forms part of a more accountable supply-chain management system for the industry in general.

Creativity, ingenuity and a passion for fibers and yarns underlie these changes. The innovations that we are seeing are driven by the consumer: by changes in consumer demographics, engagement with the environment and a growing awareness of global social responsibility. This is a time of change and change is good.

ENGINEERED FIBERS AND YARNS

The extent to which fibers and yarns can now be engineered is allowing for a dramatic increase in the development of fibers for wellness, health and protection. DuPont's Nomex branded technology protects racing drivers, firemen and others at risk from exposure to fire. Nomex is a synthetic aromatic polyamide polymer that offers high levels of electrical, chemical and mechanical integrity when converted into different sheet forms. It was first used in the mid-1960s and since then it has proved remarkably versatile. It is still employed in military and protective clothing as well as applications in airbag technologies and filtration. It is now available as a smart fiber in the patented Nomex On Demand. The fiber has the ability to expand by three or four times its size when exposed to temperatures above 121°C (250°F). To firefighters, this means an increase in protection of about 20% when the material is used as a thermal liner in their clothing; because it can remain thin and flexible under normal conditions it is more comfortable than a material that retains one bulk state throughout.

Aramids were developed in the mid-1960s using a liquid crystalline polymer solution as the basis for the fiber. The most common brand name is Kevlar, produced by DuPont. Designed to protect against cuts (including ballistic impact), abrasion and extreme heat hazards, it can be produced in several fiber forms depending on the intended use. These include pulp for use as a speciality additive in friction and sealing applications, continuous fiber or filament, and spun yarn and yarns that are further twisted and plied into cord format. Instantly recognizable by its trademark natural yellow colour, Kevlar is now being produced in a different-coloured version. It has been notoriously difficult to colour, to such an extent that some manufacturers have made a feature of this. Applications range from ballistic vests for police and military to protective gloves and chainsaw chaps. The company tests the effectiveness of Kevlar against cuts in a comparative study with cotton and leather alternatives. Testing is vitally important in protective clothing and DuPont has been at the forefront of testing facilities. Their Glove Torture Chamber is a rotating drum with razor blades attached to the inside. Equally weighted aramid, cotton and leather gloves are compared as they rotate in the drum. While both cotton and leather are badly damaged, the aramid glove is unharmed.

The Japanese company Teijin Ltd produce a para-aramid under the brand name Technora, which the company claim is eight times stronger than steel and three times stronger than fiberglass. It is an aromatic copolyamid and offers high-dimensional stability because of its stiff and highly orientated molecular structure. In tests it is shown to maintain more than half of its tensile strength at temperatures of 250°C (482°F). It is produced as filament yarn, staple fiber, short fiber and stretch-broken yarn.

One of the greatest challenges in composite construction is in achieving drape and complex curved forms without causing wrinkles. High-strength yarns such as carbon fibers and aramids tend to have little elasticity. This, along with cost, has provided the impetus behind the development of stretch-broken yarns or aligned discontinuous fibers, as they are also known. Relatively long (7.5–10 cm; 3–4 in.) fiber lengths are taken and

Stretch aramid, *Lenzi Egisto, Italy.* The manufacturer has overcome the limitations of the low-elasticity aramid yarn in this stretch fabric. This makes it more comfortable to wear, particularly over long periods of time.

Opposite and overleaf: *Aramid and polyamide production processes from CIRFS: European Man-made Fibres Association with final graphics.* Yarn and fiber production techniques often advance at a faster pace than fabric techniques. This can lead to delays in bringing new yarns to market as the fabric construction technology catches up.

held together with filaments or a binder that will allow them to move more freely without any significant reduction in strength or performance. The French manufacturer Schappe has designed their own proprietary fiber-breaking machine. In their stretch-broken carbon fiber (SBCF) carbon fibers are aligned and spun with similarly broken thermoplastic filaments to form fine commingled yarns. These are then wrapped with a continuous serving filament of the same polymer to stabilize the final yarn.

Dyneema is a polyethylene fiber that has a very high strength. The producers, DSM Dyneema, estimate its strength to be up to 15 times higher than that of a quality steel and up to 40% stronger than an aramid fiber on a weight for weight basis. The yarn is light enough to float on water, is ultraviolet (UV) resistant, durable and resistant to moisture which makes it appropriate for a range of applications from yachting to aviation. In yachting it can be found in rigging as well as in woven and membrane sails. In both instances it offers strength with low weight and the bright white of the yarn gives it a high visibility. The company has also launched Dyneema Purity as the first implantable grade ultra-high-molecular-weight polyethylene (UHMWPE) fiber. This has been followed by Dyneema Purity BLUE which sees the addition of colour to the yarn. This eliminates the need to add coloured polyester or nylon to the yarn for applications where surgeons require colour identification to help differentiate between multiple sutures during operations. The benefit of the solid colour is that it is easier to see and mark apart from a yarn with a colour strand spiralled within it.

Sustainability is behind a number of new fiber developments as manufacturers look to combine benefit to the environment with performance. In Japan, Teijin is involving the consumer directly in the production of their polyester PET fibers. Ecocircle is a closed-loop recycling system that takes polyester products at the end of their use and turns them into polyester PET fibers at the company's Matsuyama plant. The consumer is encouraged not just to buy products with the Ecocircle certification, but also to bring them to a recycling bin at a participating store or post them to Teijin direct. The company has developed a number of high-performance health-giving fibers using this process including Wellkey, Microft and Cortico. Wellkey is a specially designed hollow fiber that wicks perspiration away from the body. Microft is a high-density microfiber with a soft handle and a water-repellent finish that makes it ideal for use in sports and leisurewear. Cortico is a highly engineered triangular fiber containing small apertures on the surface to absorb perspiration more readily. When the original health-giving fabrics were first introduced a decade ago, they were strong on performance but weak on comfort and handle. We are now seeing the second generation of these fibers and fabrics with dramatically improved qualities.

New spinning technologies are revolutionizing what can be achieved in terms of performance and comfort in fibers and yarns. Electrospinning is yielding some very encouraging results in the production of nanofibers. The process takes a polymer solution and subjects it to an electrostatic charge to eject fine jets of liquid. These are then stretched in an electric field under simultaneous evaporation of the solvent. The result is a deposition of a nanofibrous nonwoven fiber mat. Fibers can be produced using either single or multiple capillary needles or by electrospinning from a liquid-free surface.

ARAMID

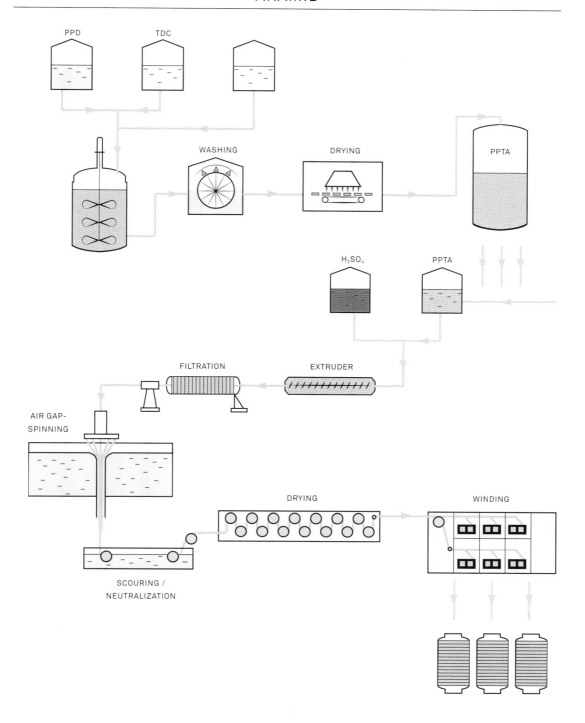

POLYAMIDE

POLYAMIDE 6 OR POLYAMIDE 6.6

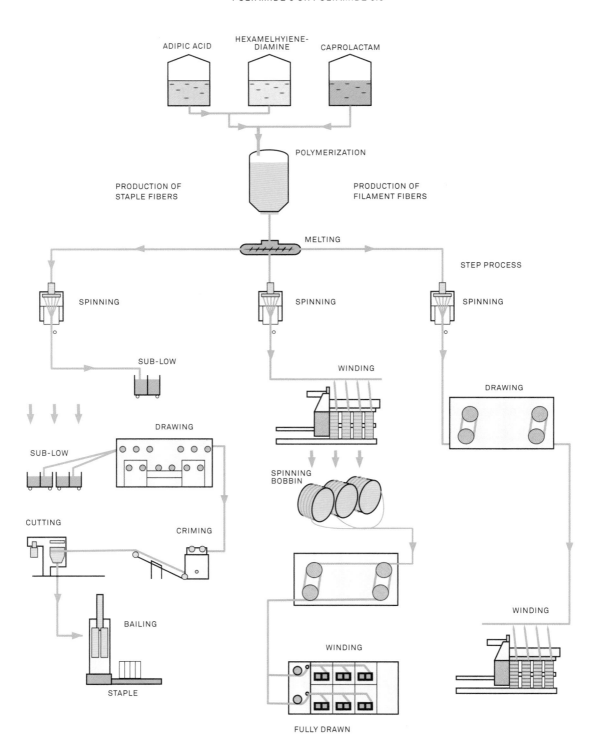

ADIPIC ACID

HEXAMELHYIENE-
DIAMINE

CAPROLACTAM

POLYMERIZATION

PRODUCTION OF
STAPLE FIBERS

PRODUCTION OF
FILAMENT FIBERS

MELTING

STEP PROCESS

SPINNING

SPINNING

SPINNING

SUB-LOW

WINDING

DRAWING

SUB-LOW

DRAWING

SPINNING
BOBBIN

CUTTING

CRIMING

WINDING

BAILING

WINDING

STAPLE

FULLY DRAWN

Vortex spinning is being used by a number of companies worldwide, including Formosa Taffeta Co. Ltd in Taiwan and the Rana Group in India. Vortex spinning sees the tip of the fiber focused on the centre of the yarn by means of a vortex of compressed air. This ensures that the centre of the yarn remains straight while a second tip forms the outer layer that twines another fiber. The resulting yarn has long and short fibers combined, with the shorter ones on the outside. The process produces yarns with inherently good moisture-absorbing properties, which are less prone to hairiness or pilling.

HYBRID YARNS

Environmental concerns are encouraging many manufacturers to focus on the use of a single fiber within their yarns; developments in engineered fibers are making this more achievable. However, there are still and will remain reasons for bringing fibers with different qualities together: particularly, for performance, health and safety applications.

The Swiss-based Schoeller Spinning Group is producing a number of aramid-based hybrid fibers. Their 30% Kevlar and 70% Panox is one example. Panox is a pre-oxidized acrylic fiber suited for heat resistant, thermal and acoustic insulation in technical textiles. The combination of the two fibers means that the resulting yarn has the cut and abrasion resistance of the aramid alongside the heat protection of the pre-oxidized acrylic. Applications include clothing for the fire services and motorcyclists. While these fibers are integrated to form the yarn, a mix of 40% Kevlar and 60% viscose sees the aramid as core and viscose as a surrounding sheath. This gives a better handle to the fiber and allows it to be dyed more easily. The Schoeller Spinning Group is using an aramid stretch-broken fiber in the core of another protective yarn. Here the core is comprised of 10% Kevlar and 50% glass filament with the Kevlar 40% sheath surround. This is used as a backing for aluminized protective suits and cut-resistant protective clothing.

The process of melt spinning can allow substances to be incorporated more fully into fibers and yarns. Thermoplastic polymer chips are first melted and fed through a spinneret using a rotating extruder screw to produce polymer threads that can then be solidified by applying a stream of cold air. This is especially important for precision yarns in areas such as medicine. Speciality Fibers and Materials Ltd is using this process to incorporate barium sulfate into a polypropylene yarn. Barium sulfate is a white crystalline solid already being used clinically to provide radio contrast in X-rays. It is usually administered to the patient orally. Micropake is an X-ray detectable yarn that can be used in woven and nonwoven products such as surgical gauze. The yarn contains 40 fibers with 60% barium sulphate. The crystalline solid is insoluble in water and would be extremely difficult to apply to a yarn using more conventional coating or finishing processes.

A category of hybrid compounds is starting to emerge. Though not a fiber in the conventional sense, they most closely resemble a yarn or fiber in that they contain a central textile component and because of the manner in which they are used. The material is produced in a form such as pellets or beads, too small to be used individually, which can only perform when used in bulk. Teijin uses this material as the basis for tyre reinforcement. It interacts with the carbon black surfaces during mixing, going on to stabilize the sulphur cross-links that form during the vulcanization process. The aramid used is Teijin's Twaron brand, where the chemical structure has been altered to allow the sulphur component to be utilized in the formation of the cross-linked compound. Sulfron (a modified aramid) has the effect of strengthening the usually unstable polysulfide cross-links, resulting in a flexible yet strong network that is not prone to rapid degradation. It is produced in granular form and typically mixed with fillers that contain synthetic rubbers.

COATED FIBERS AND YARNS

While the majority of coatings and treatments are applied to the finished fabric, there is an increasing trend to apply these treatments to fibers and yarns. This is generally for high-performance and specialist applications, but as costs come down there is likely to be an increase in demand and availability.

The Schoeller Spinning Group is responding to the demand for comfort combined with high performance in their development of a wool and stainless steel yarn for anti-static clothing. The yarn in cross-section shows 92% Merino wool randomly interspersed with 8% Inox stainless steel fiber. The yarn can be easily dyed and knitted and is capable of being finished with treatments such as Teflon without interfering with the shielding performance. The ability to combine several capabilities in a single yarn is relatively new. Less than a decade ago this would not have been possible without reducing, or even destroying, the performance of one or both functionalities.

Nanocoatings have made progress largely in fabrics, but are starting to appear on the individual fibers. Researchers at Cornell University's Textiles Nanotechnology Laboratory have developed a way of coating fibers with polyelectrolytes, inorganic and metallic nanolayers, to develop specialist high-performance and smart materials. Developments include

Bekinox LT, *Bekaert, Belgium.*
These slivers of stainless steel fibers can be used on their own or combined with other fibers for anti-static applications such as in carpets.

Hinoki, *Grado Zero Espace, Italy.* The raw material is extracted from the bark of the Eastern Cypress tree and is noted for its soothing scent along with deodorizing properties and mildew prevention. It is produced in a blend with 50% cotton.

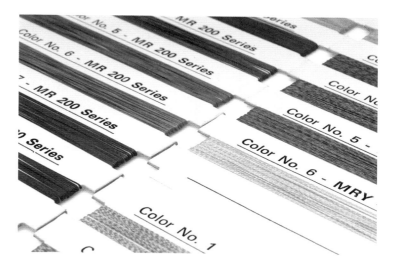

a cotton coated with silver and gold nanoparticles. In this process cotton is positively charged using ammonium- and epoxy-based reactions to induce positive ionization. The silver or gold particles, about 10nm in diameter, are synthesized in citric acid, which prevents nanoparticles colliding and sticking together. In dipping the positively charged cotton into the negatively charged metal nanoparticle solution the silver or gold particles cling to the cotton fibers. The benefit of the process is to produce an anti-bacterial yarn that destroys bacteria and reduces the need for washing. In a separate development by the same team, nylon nanofibers have been coated with gold nanoparticles and anomalous crystal formations of NaC(R) for potential applications in the active filtration of hazardous gases and toxic chemicals as well as anti-counterfeiting devices.

Researchers at the Georgia Institute of Technology are looking at ways to optimize the collection of solar energy. The majority of systems rely on flat panels directed at the sun either as static systems or capable of rotating to follow the direction of the sun's rays. At Georgia they are researching how to create a PV (photovoltaic) fiber that can be woven into the membrane. To achieve this they are nanocoating fiber optics with a dye-sensitized photovoltaic coating. The cladding of the fiber optic is removed and replaced with a conductive coating and seed layer of zinc oxide. Zinc oxide nanowire is then grown on this prepared surface so that the result is a coating of fur nanowires. This is coated with a dye-sensitized PV material before being immersed in liquid electrolyte to collect current from the photovoltaic reaction. The ends of the fiber are directed at the sun: light enters the unclad fiber optic carrying it along and through the wall to the nano PV so that it covers a very large area. Researchers are confident that it will prove much more efficient than conventional systems of collection.

Sweden's Swerea IVF is developing a process for coating microfibers with nanofibers. The aim is to use the fibers to create scaffolding for tissue engineering based on the principles of collagen. Initial studies have shown that the adhesion and proliferation of the microfiber is greatly enhanced by the addition of the nanofiber coating. The nanofiber coating is applied

Promix milk protein fiber and copper,
Nuno, Japan. Developed by Reiko Sudo at Nuno, this fabric is given a slightly pink tint caused by including copper in the weave. The contemporary interest in milk protein fibers in textiles originated in Japan, where both manufacturers and designers such as Reiko Sudo at Nuno did much to develop and refine the fiber.

by the use of a grounded collector that rotates around the microfiber. As the collector rotates, an electric field is applied, which forces the nanofibers to collide with, and be deposited on, the microfiber. The nanofiber-coated microfibers are then taken to the next stage and formed into the scaffold.

TECHNONATURALS

Much of the development of the technonaturals has been driven by the apparel market. Lessons have been learnt from the early development of health-giving, highly engineered fibers in the 1990s where performance was high but tactile qualities low. In combining natural with synthetic, or creating hypernaturals, these new yarns look to combine the best of both worlds, delivering performance with good tactile qualities.

The Lenzing Group's key product is lyocell, a cellulose fiber made from wood pulp sold under the trade name Tencel. The wood pulp is converted into nanofibrils using nanotechnology so that the result is an exceptionally fine yarn that offers high moisture management with good tactile properties. Tencel absorbs excess liquid and then quickly releases it into the atmosphere to help to keep the body at a comfortable temperature. This function carries an additional anti-bacterial benefit because, since excess water is moved away from the skin, bacteria have less opportunity to grow. The smooth surface of the yarn makes it pleasant to wear and gives the cloth a good handle and drape. Used in conjunction with aramid fibers, it provides high fire protection with comfort, especially important in firefighting workwear where clothing has to be worn for prolonged periods of time under stressful conditions.

Smartfiber AG produce a lyocell fiber, SeaCell, with enhanced health properties. It uses seaweed as an active ingredient in the lyocell fiber. Seaweed has long been used in Chinese medicine and is recognized as offering protection for the skin; it also contains anti-inflammatory properties. There is what is termed an 'active exchange' between the fiber and the skin. The company describes how there is an exchange of substances between the fiber and the skin with nutrients such as calcium, magnesium and vitamin E released by the body's natural moisture when a garment using the fiber is worn. Algae is particularly good at absorbing metals. This has prompted a second version of the fiber, SeaCell active plus, which sees silver ions added for anti-bacterial benefits.

Milk cotton fabric, *Technical Fabric Services (TFS), Australia.* Milk protein fiber is combined with equal quantities of cotton and a small percentage of elastane for fabrics that retain their whiteness and remain bright over repeated washings.

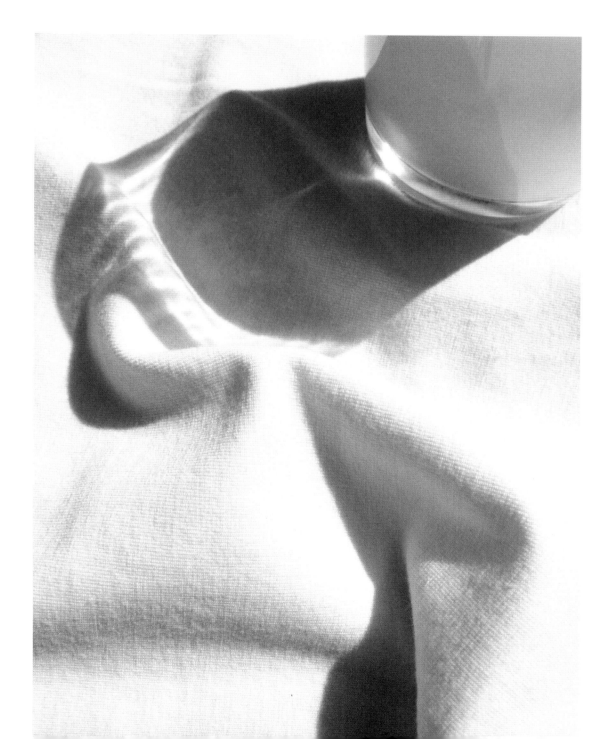

***Cocona fiber**, Cocona Inc., USA, 2009.* Cocona activated carbon is manufactured from coconut waste and absorbs odour and offers UV protection. It is not depleted during washing or wearing because it is embedded in the fiber.

***Bamboo charcoal neoprene**, Rip Curl, Australia, 2008.* The iconic Australian surf label continually evaluates the fabrics it uses both in terms of performance and environmental criteria. This sample combines the anti-bacterial properties of bamboo and the odour absorption of charcoal.

The idea of dressing in milk carries connotations of living like Queen Cleopatra of Egypt, who bathed in milk. It is undoubtedly one of the attractions of clothes made from milk protein fiber. Milk protein, or casein, has its origin as a binder in paints where it offered superior whiteness and remained bright over long periods of time. Used in textiles today, it is obtained from skimmed, evaporated and condensed milk, yielding around three pounds of casein to every hundred of milk. The yarn is produced by chemically treating the casein and then extruding it through a series of spinnerets. It is combined with other fibers such as cotton and synthetics to which it brings additional comfort and moisture-absorbing qualities. It is particularly popular for applications in intimate apparel and is being used by companies such as Technical Fabric Services (TFS) Australia in fabric made for AussieBum.

Seaweed forms the basis for a new range of wound dressings that are highly absorbent, encouraging faster healing. The British company Speciality Fibres and Materials Ltd is extracting the raw material from seaweed in order to produce alginate fibers. Hydrophilic polymers are extracted from the seaweed and produced as a powder in the soluble, sodium form. The sodium alginate is then dissolved in water before being extruded into a bath solution of calcium ions. This process allows the formation of continuous filaments that can then be stretched, washed, dried and crimped before being cut into short lengths for further processing, usually as a nonwoven wound dressing. The fiber combines fluid absorption with gel formation to provide dressings that keep the wound at the right degree of dryness to encourage healing and reduce the patient's pain.

Advanced production processes are making it possible to work with non-textile materials to convert them into yarns. This has the advantage of combining the flexibility of a yarn with the performance of ceramic and metals. Smartcel Ceramic is made by Smartfiber AG and brings together cellulose and ceramic resulting in a 100% ceramic fiber. The core technology of smartcel is made from a cellulose using a modified ALCERU patented manufacturing process from the Thuringian Institute of Textile and Plastics Research (TITK). The Smartcel Ceramic can be produced in different forms including hollow and spiral structures; the choice is driven by the end application. A sintered PZT ceramic fiber has the ability to stretch when exposed to alternating voltage-producing soundwaves in the process. This gives it an application in ultrasound products such as sonar systems for locating obstructions and medical imaging.

Medicinal properties have long been attributed to germanium, so much so that in the city of Da-Lian in China the municipal water is often referred to as miracle holy water because of its germanium content. Generic germanium exists deep underground or within other elements such as water. The Taiwanese manufacturer Formosa Taffeta Co. Ltd is producing a germanium yarn that sees the element embedded in the yarn. Sun Dream Enterprise Co. Ltd is manufacturing germanium alloy yarns through the use of high-temperature sintering

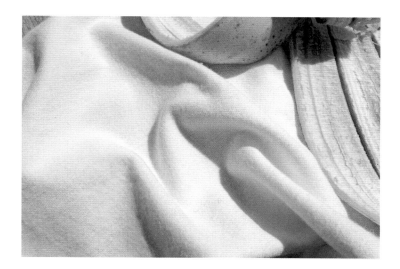

Banana cotton fabric, *Technical Fabric Services (TFS), Australia.* Banana fibers in textiles offer a sustainable product that is highly absorbent. Fibers are extracted from the bark of the plant and then combined with cotton and elastane for comfort and stretch in fabrics for intimate apparel.

and nanogrinding. These convert the alloy into an alloy crystal that can then be encapsulated within the fiber. Both manufacturers also produce Anion fibers. Sun Dream Enterprise market their product under the brand name Anion (negative ion) Air Vitamin. The intention is also to create a greater sense of wellbeing, reducing tiredness, improving circulation and enhancing the body's immune system. An anion is a negatively charged ion and commonly found in health-marketed watches and bracelets.

Using waste materials that might otherwise go to landfill is an ambition that is motivating the development of innovative fibers, including technonaturals. The American manufacturer Cocona Inc. is producing a fiber that offers UV protection and odour resistance, while utilizing a plant material that would otherwise go straight to landfill. Cocona technology takes the discarded shell of the coconut and converts it into an activated carbon that is then embedded in fibers such as polyester and nylon during production. It is being combined with other yarns for apparel such as Merino wool where it brings a fast-drying property to the product.

The use of bamboo fiber has attracted a great deal of attention, both positive and negative. On the one hand, it can be grown without the use of heavy pesticides and has been shown to have anti-bacterial characteristics, but balanced against this is the difficulty in regulating the fiber to differentiate between the mechanical and the chemically processed fiber, the correct term for the latter being bamboo rayon. As regulators increase the pressure for correct labelling, manufacturers are turning to accredited, world-recognized organizations such as Oeko-Tex to certify the provenance of their yarns and fibers. In China the Ningbo GuangYuan Fabric Co. Ltd is producing a bamboo carbon fiber. The aim of the fiber is to promote health and general wellbeing in its use in apparel. The fiber is made by the addition of a bamboo carbon nanopowder to a viscose solution as the yarn is spun. The resulting yarn is odour-absorbing and deodorizing because of the activated carbon element and anti-bacterial due to the bamboo component. The yarn is used in knitted fabrics either on its own or in combination with other yarns such as cotton.

NANOTECHNOLOGY

Nanotechnology is at a relatively young stage of development with much of the work still at research stage. Advances are being made in many areas such as the production of high-strength carbon nanotubes, but scale and the cost of production still have to be overcome in order to make it a viable manufacturing process. Nanotubes, as the name suggests, are a tube-shaped material made from carbon atoms bound together to create a stiff structure that forms the strongest existing bond. They can be classed as single-walled, double-walled or multi-walled. To be classed as nano the diameter has to measure on the nanometer (nm) scale, which is around one ten thousandth the thickness of a human hair.

Nanocyl are a Belgian company who specialize in the production of carbon nanotubes. Nanocyl use a catalytic carbon vapour deposition production method because of its reliability and ability to produce on a relatively large scale. Large-scale in nano terms means a measurement in centimetres. Single-walled nanotubes (SWNT) have a single cylindrical graphite wall and come in the form of tubes that are capped at either end. The structure is visualized as a graphite layer just one atom thick, referred to as graphene, which has been rolled into a seamless cylinder. SWNTs are typically 1nm in diameter, but much longer in length. They are pliable and can be twisted, bent and flattened without breaking. The nanotubes also display a unique set of electrical and mechanical properties, giving them a wide range of applications including nanocomposites and nanosensors. Nanocyl are working in partnership with 3B-Fiberglass on the development of a CNT (carbon nanotube)-sized glass fiber for thermoplastic and structural composites. The intention is to combine the two technologies and joint performances so that the resulting fibers will be mechanically strong and electrically conductive.

One possible means of reducing the cost and increasing scale is to use carbon nanotubes as fillers. Researchers at Swerea IVF are investigating this possibility as a way of producing conductive yarns. In one method a polyolefin is blended with an electrically conductive carbon nanotube and carbon black filler using a melt spinning process. The filler content is limited by the viscosity: the greater the number of contact points, the higher the viscosity and conductivity. To achieve this, particles have to be coated with a conducting material so that the resistance of each contact point can be lowered.

Biomimetics, the extraction of good design from nature, is proving an inspiration in the area of nanotechnology. Teijin took the idea of their Morphotex fiber from the wings of the Morpho butterfly whose vivid blue iridescent colour is the result of microscopic scales on the backs of the wings. In flight, the butterfly appears and then disappears, camouflaged against the blue of the sky. Looking to create a yarn that can morph and change in response to its environment, Teijin has created a filament yarn using nanotechnology. It is engineered to produce colour without the need for dyes. The fabric has been used by the Australian fashion designer Donna Sgro in her Octopus Garden collection.

BIOTECHNOLOGY, GENETICALLY MODIFIED
ORGANISMS (GMO) AND SYNTHETIC BIOLOGY

Biotechnology refers to any technological application that uses biological systems, living organisms or their derivatives to make or modify products or processes. A number of developments in this area are aimed at producing fibers that are sustainable as well as high in performance.

Polylactic acid (PLA) is a linear aliphatic thermoplastic polyester that is derived from 100% renewable sources such as corn. It offers good moisture control, UV and anti-microbial protection while being compostable. Two companies have been behind the development and refinement of the technology and its use in textile applications, Kanebo Cosmetics Inc. in Japan and NatureWorks LLC in America. Kanebo's fiber is marketed under the trade name Lactron while NatureWorks' PLA uses the trade name Ingeo. The Taiwanese company Jeen Wei Enterprise Co. Ltd is also using PLA to make narrow-width webbing.

Dr Tara Sutherland and her colleagues at Australia's Commonwealth Scientific and Industrial Research Organisation (CSIRO) have developed an artificial honeybee silk that offers toughness alongside an ability to absorb energy. In the process, fine threads of honeybee silk are hand drawn from a 'soup' of silk proteins that have been produced transgenically. Recombinant cells of bacterium E. coli are used to produce the silk proteins that can then go on to self-assemble into a structure similar to the silk produced naturally. Because of its scale and biocompatibility, end uses are expected in medical applications such as sutures, artificial tendons and ligaments.

For the growing medical and healthcare industry, researchers at the Technion Israel Institute of Technology are looking to use bovine serum albumin, a protein found in cow's blood, to create threads that will offer a significant reduction in the scarring caused by stitches. The globular molecules in the protein have the ability to form long, even fibers when combined with beta-mercaptoethanol in an electrospinning process. An added benefit of the albumin is that its glue-like properties help to stick torn tissue together and encourage the healing process.

Morphotex, *Teijin Ltd, Japan.* The inspiration for the fiber comes from the Morpho butterfly which uses optic effects to provide protective camouflage in the Amazon rainforest. The fiber is produced using nanotechnology.

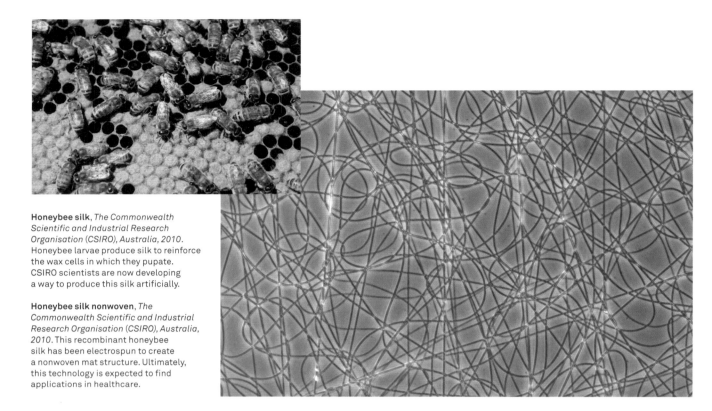

Honeybee silk, *The Commonwealth Scientific and Industrial Research Organisation (CSIRO), Australia, 2010.* Honeybee larvae produce silk to reinforce the wax cells in which they pupate. CSIRO scientists are now developing a way to produce this silk artificially.

Honeybee silk nonwoven, *The Commonwealth Scientific and Industrial Research Organisation (CSIRO), Australia, 2010.* This recombinant honeybee silk has been electrospun to create a nonwoven mat structure. Ultimately, this technology is expected to find applications in healthcare.

The California-based Genomatica Inc. is part of a new breed of biotechnology developer who describe themselves as a sustainable chemicals company. Scientists there have found a way of producing plastic and thermoplastic fibers using sugar and water rather than oil. They have developed strains of bacteria that can produce butanediol (BDO) using predominantly sugar and water. BDO can be manufactured into plastics and fibers with a combination of specialized computational modelling, a wet lab for microbe modification and chemical processing engineering.

GENETICALLY MODIFIED ORGANISMS (GMO)

Genetically modified organisms (GMO) are organisms whose genetic material has been altered using the process of genetic engineering. DNA molecules from different sources are generally used with a technique referred to as recombinant DNA technology. The molecules are combined into one to create a new set of genes that are then transferred into an organism to give it new or modified genes. The technology is highly controversial. There are concerns about its long-term effect on humans and the environment, including its impact on non-GM crops. A further issue is the existence of the terminator gene technology that allows one-use only seeds that are genetically modified to prevent seeds being generated for use the following year which is normal farming practice for many crops. The latter is seen as being particularly hard on poor farmers in developing countries. However, there are also a great number of potential benefits, so that many countries and even states within countries remain undecided about whether or not to ban the technology and its products.

Monsanto is at the forefront of GM seed research and development. They introduced the first GM cotton, Ingard, in 1996, followed more recently by Bollgard II. The development sees bacterium *Bacillus thuringiensis* (Bt) inserted into the cotton. These, in turn, develop two proteins that are toxic to just one insect, the Helicoverpa caterpillar, who is the crop's main pest. Preliminary test results suggest that the crop may also require less water than conventional cotton and offer an 80% reduction in the use of pesticides compared with conventional crops, thus cutting down on contamination of the waterways. Monsanto is currently developing new water use efficiency (WUE) and nitrogen use efficiency (NUE) traits aimed at further conservation of water and nitrogen. In Australia, CSIRO is using gene technology to breed genetically modified insect-resistant and herbicide-resistant CSIRO cotton varieties using Bollgard II and Roundup Ready Flex traits from Monsanto.

Synthetic life or synthetic biology refer to the design of biological systems that do not already exist in nature. With their basis in genetic engineering, these are, in effect, living machines that have the potential to be smart and responsive, and able to replicate and even mutate. It is this last area, in particular, that causes concern and a call for global regulation. It is regarded by experts as technically feasible to replicate the smallpox virus, one of the most devastating diseases in human history, for instance. It also has the potential to help tackle climate change and lead to a replacement for fossil fuels. They may also form the basis for a new smart textile or fabric coating.

There are two approaches to the technology. The first involves the use of standard biological building blocks referred to as BioBricks which encode basic biological functions. These could be designed to meet different criteria: to operate at extreme temperatures or soak up carbon dioxide, for example. Researchers at MIT, Harvard and the University of California, San Francisco (UCSF) have set up the BioBricks Foundation (BBF), a not-for-profit organization that encourages research and development in this area. The BioBricks standard biological parts are available to scientists free on MIT's Registry of Standard Biological Parts. While this is at a very early stage of development, the technology could ultimately have applications in developing new fibers.

Dr Craig Venter and his team at the J. Craig Venter Institute (JCVI) in California are working in a very different way. In May 2010 the institute announced their success in creating their first self-replicating synthetic bacterial cell. It had taken fifteen years. The synthetic cell is called Mycoplasma mycoides JCVI-syn1.0 and is intended to demonstrate that computer-designed genomes can go on to be chemically made in the laboratory before being transplanted into a recipient cell. This cell would proceed to produce a new self-replicating cell, which would be controlled only by the synthetic genome. Fibers of the future may literally have a life of their own.

Genetically modified (GM) cotton, Monsanto, USA. The debate on the merits versus dangers of GM looks set to continue as the textile industry moves towards greater accountability in supply-chain management.

FABRIC STRUCTURES

Multi-axial weave, *RWTH Aachen, Germany.* Two different glass fibers have been used in these multi-axial weaves. The material is used for industrial applications where high strength and flame retardancy are required.

The possibilities offered by the structural formation of fabrics would appear to be endless. Knitted and woven fabrics can combine a vast array of yarns and be used to create both two- and three-dimensional fabrics. Nonwovens, an informal matrix of fibers bound together, have become a more robust material capable of incorporating a great number of performance benefits. Stitch or embroidery has gone beyond the decorative and is now being used to produce some of the most intricate materials that simply would not be possible using any other textile process. Finally, there is the possibility of composites where two or more materials are brought together to create a third new material with enhanced capabilities.

The structures in this section gain their performance through three main criteria. The first is the selection of yarns and fibers; these can be a single type or use two or more to combine characteristics, add visual and tactile qualities or reduce costs. In the second case the structure of the fabric provides the performance and the choice of yarn is secondary, often a polyester for its flexibility. The third sees the combination of fiber choice and structure. The designers and manufacturers in this section are increasingly approaching their work as a dialogue to produce the best fabric possible for the application. Boundaries are being pushed, limits stretched, as the potential of the structure of textiles comes under scrutiny as never before.

WEAVE

Woven fabrics, whether flat or three-dimensional, display great versatility. Their strength allows textiles to be used on vastly different scales. Large applications, in particular, are finding a place for textiles where they offer a lightweight alternative to heavier materials. The space industry's automated transfer vehicle (ATV) uses a woven aramid fiber from Bexco for its cables. Bringing space technology back to earth, the Italian company Grado Zero Espace incorporate a shape memory metal into their woven fabric for Oricalco shirts to enable them to change shape according to temperature. The incorporation of conductive yarns into woven fabrics is an area of continued refinement. Bayer MaterialScience AG is combining CNT-coated electro conductive fiber (CNTEC) – conductive yarns produced by Kuraray Living Co. Ltd – with their own Baytubes carbon nanotubes (CNTs) in a woven textile. The CNTs allow for high electrical and thermal conductivity. The fabric is anti-freezing and can be used in clothing, car seats and other applications.

Reiko Sudo at Nuno has worked with the Tsuruoka Weaving Cooperative on her kibiso-based fabrics. The kibiso outer portion of the silk cocoon was previously discarded as waste, useful only in protecting the finer silk beneath. It is sometimes used as a natural amino acid in non-textile industries such as cosmetics and pet food manufacture. The material has now been found to provide, in a natural form, qualities that are useful for clothing, such as moisture and UV filtration. In *Kibiso Bookshelf* and *Futsu Crisscross*, the Japanese designer combines the material with their natural materials such as raw silk and cotton. The weaving process brings together the handmade (the kibiso fiber must be split by hand) and the technical

Kibiso, *Nuno, Japan, 2010*.
Reiko Sudo in collaboration with the
Tsuruoka Weaving Cooperative have
developed a way of using sericin-rich
silk cocoon waste to make a fabric
that offers UV protection.

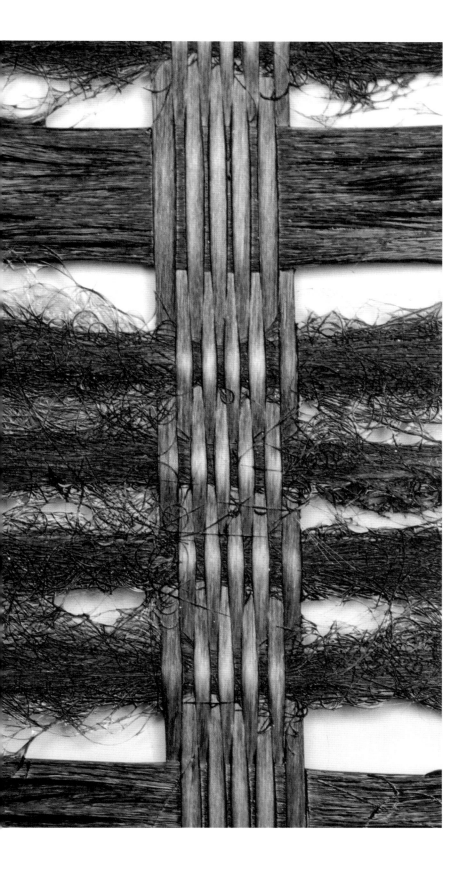

in the final weaving of the cloth. Changes in weather patterns mean that seasons are shifting and temperatures rising. One of the consequences is the impact this has on plants and crops. Many now need protection, especially from the heat of the sun. Hortisynthetics are a group of fabrics that provide ground cover for plants without interfering with their access to light and ability to grow. In India, Shri Ambica Polymer is producing the Ambica range of hortisynthetic fabrics. These are black woven polypropylene fabrics designed to provide UV protection and weed control for plants at a low cost.

The Swiss textile manufacturer Schoeller Spinning Group produce high-performance fabrics for a number of markets including sports and leisurewear. Metallic fibers and finishes are appearing regularly in their collections. Metal and metal-alloy-coated yarns are introduced to the weave to give the fabrics a 'memory'. This means they can be formed by hand into a three-dimensional shape and then flattened to their original state. Coatings and finishing treatments are additional technical and aesthetic qualities that can be given to the woven fabric.

Yuxin woven polyester geogrid, Shandong Shenghao Fiberglass Co. Ltd, China. The company use both polyester and glass fiber in their range of geogrids with yarn coatings that include bitumen and PVC. The fabric is used for reinforcement in roads, railways and bridges.

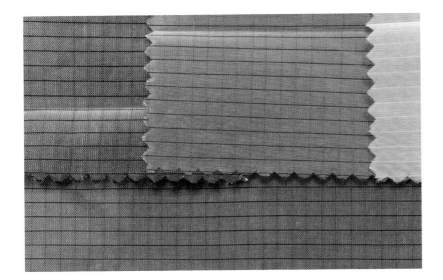

Ripstop weave with synthetic and metal, Schoeller Textiles AG, Switzerland. Metallic alloy fibers are introduced to the weave to allow the fabric to be formed and shaped, bringing a high-tech aesthetic to the performance fabric.

KNIT

While the idea of a functionally gradient material has been considered for some time, it has until recently been largely confined to the composites or used as an aesthetic in the fashion industry. The combined impetus of performance and sustainability has meant that sportswear and lingerie are showing interest in this area. It offers the chance to produce garments using a single material in one process. WarmX, for example, produce climate-control underwear using a number of materials and processes, including a variable knitted structure. The company's design for SilverSun is based on body-mapping principles. The intention is to provide the optimum in comfort and warmth aimed at the outdoor market. A silver-plated yarn is used in areas where perspiration is likely, so as to reduce odour and combat bacteria, while an elasticated hybrid yarn is used for the main body of the garment to ensure that heat is evenly distributed around the body. Office chairs were revolutionized by the advent of the Aeron Chair from Herman Miller. Acclaimed by both the design press and consumers, its patented mesh fabric proved that layers of foam and wadding were not necessary to produce a comfortable and ergonomic chair. Numerous companies have followed suit, including advanced knitting specialists Kobleder in Austria. The company is part of the next generation in contract furnishing fabrics, producing functionally gradient ergonomic fabric for seating. Using the flame-retardant Trevira CS multifilament, they are producing fabric for chair designers as well as prototype aircraft seating, offering a considerable weight saving compared with conventional seats.

Flat-bed and three-dimensional knitting are being used on vastly different scales. On the one hand, there are medical implants and devices for cornea surgery, as prototyped by RWTH Aachen. In Japan the Asahi Kasei Fibers Corporation is producing Cubit, a spacer fabric that has been engineered with a diagonal brace produced using a double raschel knit. It provides cushioning support with ventilation in applications such as wheelchairs and car seating.

Prototype of a functionally gradient knit. Materials that can vary their stretch, strength and consequently their functionality are allowing designers to avoid unnecessary seams and produce garments in a single-yarn type.

Cornea implant, RWTH Aachen, Germany. Prototype three-dimensional knitted polyester textile designed for delicate cornea implant medical procedures.

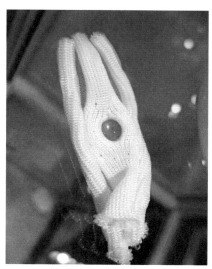

Spacer fabrics, *Heathcoat, UK.*
Polyester knitted spacer fabric
(above and seen in section opposite,
top). These provide cushioning
and ventilation in a wide range
of applications from luggage and
trainers to clothing.

Visibility and flame retardancy are common requirements
in protective clothing. The Dutch company Concordia Textiles
NV has launched a Flamacryl fabric range that can combine
both for use in protective workwear. The basic fabric includes
a combination of Protex, the inherently flame-retardant
acrylic yarn, cotton for good tactile qualities and a Nega-stat
anti-static yarn. The fabric can be produced in a high visibility
orange. The material is intended for workers in the electricity
and petrochemical industries and others at risk, though not
for firefighters. The anti-static core conducting yarns protect
the wearer from electric arcs and prevent the garments from
being electrostatically charged.

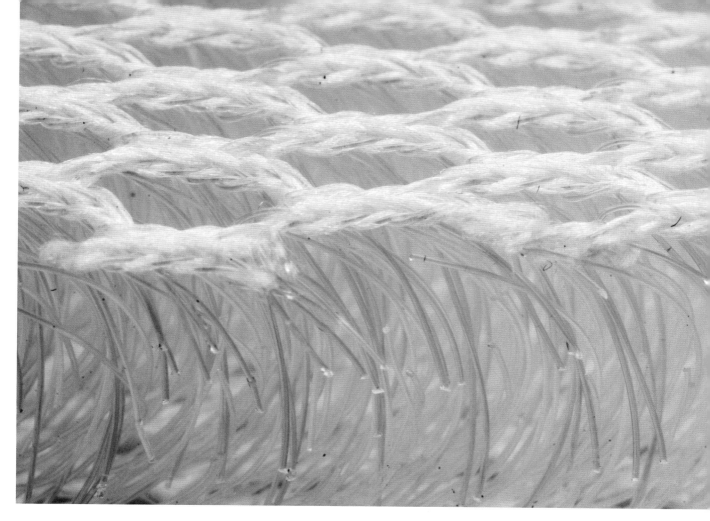

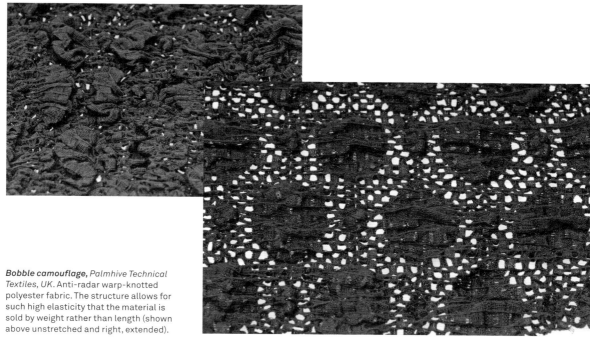

Bobble camouflage, *Palmhive Technical Textiles, UK.* Anti-radar warp-knotted polyester fabric. The structure allows for such high elasticity that the material is sold by weight rather than length (shown above unstretched and right, extended).

Metal cube, *Fraunhofer Institute for Manufacturing Technology and Advanced Materials (IFAM), Germany.* Prototype stainless steel foam cube for applications in heat, energy and acoustic insulation.

Ceramic foam, *Fairey Industrial Ceramics, UK.* Ceramic foam made using a synthetic foam that is then eliminated during the firing process to leave a product that is 100% ceramic.

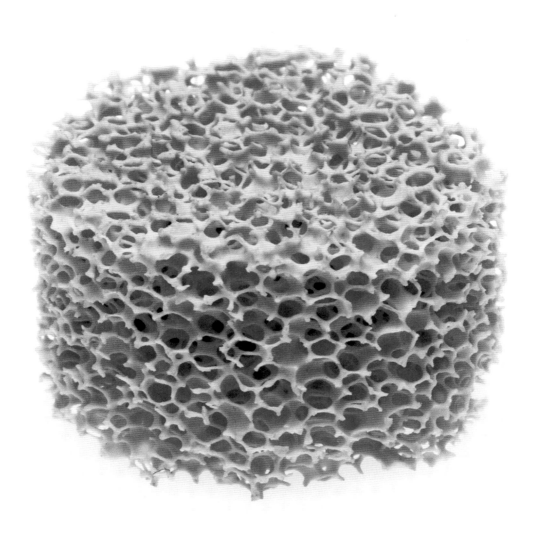

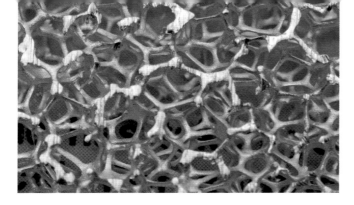

Duocel, *ERG Materials and Aerospace Corporation, USA.* This is an open networked porous aluminium foam structure with interconnected open-cell chambers. The size of the pores and density are made to specification for the aerospace industry.

FOAM

Bayer MaterialScience AG is manufacturing foams for energy absorption which are specifically aimed at the automotive market to protect occupants in the event of collision. Bayfill EA is a polyurethane (PU) foam that can be moulded to shape and used in both car interiors and exteriors. It is a low-density, semi-rigid foam. The Dow Chemical Company produce IMPAXX, an extruded thermoplastic foam that absorbs energy on impact and is also used for vibration damping. It is low density and closed cell in structure. It can be used for automotive interiors and is recyclable.

A number of foam structures are being produced using non-textile materials such as metal or ceramic. Foamet combines the material performance of metal with the structural advantage of foam. The foam is produced in Germany by Hollomet GmbH and uses a powder metallurgical manufacturing process to produce open-celled foams using a variety of sinterable metal powder. An organic carrier is first coated with a metal powder binder suspension, with the carrier material removed by heat during the manufacturing. Sintering completes the process to reveal a highly permeable material with large specific surface and low specific density, making it suitable for applications in filtration and products for thermal insulation and heat exchangers. The American company ERG Materials and Aerospace Corporation also produce a metal foam, Duocel. It is manufactured using a technique of directional solidification of the metal from a superheated liquid state. This is carried out in a controlled over-pressure and high-vacuum environment. The rectangular open foam has duodecahedronal-shaped cells that are connected by continuous metal ligaments. The pattern of the rigid structure is regular and repeatable so that the density is controllable. It is used in industrial and aerospace applications such as heat shielding for aircraft exhausts.

As wearable technologies become increasingly integrated, all areas of textile structures are being developed in this area and foam is no exception. The Adaptive Information Cluster at Dublin City University (DCU) is looking at the development of foam-based sensors for wearable sensing. An open-cell polyurethane foam is coated with polypyrrole (PPy) by a soaking and polymerization process. The coated foam is conductive without compromising the soft, compressible mechanical properties of the original foam substrate. This is especially important given the proximity to the body and the need to maintain wearer comfort and a pleasant tactile quality. It exhibits a piezoresistive reaction when it is exposed to an electrical current. The foam has been used in a prototype vest where it can measure breathing, scapula pressure, shoulder and neck movement. The intention is that the technology can be used in medical garments for patient monitoring, but it could also have applications in computing and sportswear.

NONWOVENS

Informal structures in synthetic and hybrid textiles have generally been referred to as nonwovens. To produce a nonwoven, yarns or fibers are loosely laid before being bonded by heat, pressure, adhesives, water, stitch or combinations of these processes. Historically, nonwovens have primarily been used as a low-cost disposable material. However, the ability to produce higher strength materials has improved their longevity and the range of applications for which they are suitable.

Healthcare, where there is a need for disposable products, is a primary user of nonwovens. The use of facemasks for filtration has extended from workers in industry to consumer use in preventing the spread of colds and flu viruses. The Daiwabo Co. Ltd and the Avian Influenza Research Centre at Kyoto Sangyo University have collaborated to develop a nonwoven facemask designed to block harmful viruses. The Aller Catcher mask uses a flat-pleated nonwoven and has both anti-virus and allergen-absorption properties and is biodegradable.

3D nonwoven, Volz Luftfilter GmbH, Germany. A glass fiber nonwoven for use in paint or ink separation during application. It is used in automotive and industrial applications.

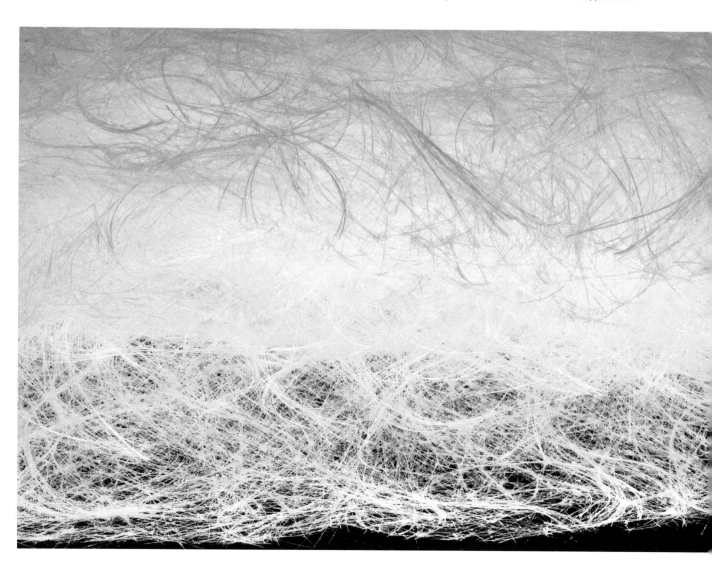

Nonwovens also have a role to play in the composites industry. Shaped three-dimensional nonwovens are used for specialist composite prepregs where high accuracy is essential. The French manufacturer Schappe has developed MAC102, a double layer, multi-axial, carbon fiber tape fabric that is made by stitching unidirectional stretch-broken tape, drawing the needles back and forth many times. In doing this, the broken ends are pulled in a 'z' direction and entangled to create a three-dimensional preform. This has been shown to provide good drapability, and mechanical and interlaminar sheer strength. In the production of composites a resin matrix is commingled with the reinforcing fibers so that prepreg can be easily moulded using processes such as compression moulding, cold stamping and bladder moulding.

Heat-protective nonwovens are produced by the HKO Heat Protection Group. Needlemats are used for the basic material and these can be further stitch-bonded or finished with an aluminized foil or adhesive backing. They can provide insulation for catalytic converters, act as exhaust silencers or a heat protection shield. The Italian company Italfeltro specialize in synthetic felts or nonwovens for applications that include the automotive and furnishing industries. Polypropylene and polyester fibers are used in a thermo-processed needled felt with performance characteristics which include being hydrophilic, anti-static, UV resistant and flame retardant. Further processing to enhance performance and aesthetics can include embossing and printing.

Autofelt, *Hassan Group, Turkey.* Recycled nonwoven using needle-punched technique for use in the automotive industry for heat and sound insulation.

Recover, The Smith Family, Australia. Recycled poly/cotton with polypropylene bonding fiber that degrades under UV, with cotton retaining moisture. Application in weed, soil and erosion control designed to biodegrade over a three-year period.

Toray Advanced Materials Korea Inc. is producing spunbond nonwovens for agricultural use in applications such as rice seedbeds and mushroom farming. The fabric is sold in specially wide widths up to 5.2 m (17 ft). Designed to be both tough and durable in harsh sunlight, the nonwovens can be treated with photostabilizers to absorb UV light. These products can also be treated with hydrophilic agents, allowing them to absorb moisture. Layering provides thickness and adds to the strength and longevity as well as the thermal insulating properties. The nonwovens are also designed to allow good air permeability so that they can maintain the proper temperature inside a tunnel or greenhouse while controlling humidity to avoid crop damage from plant disease or insects.

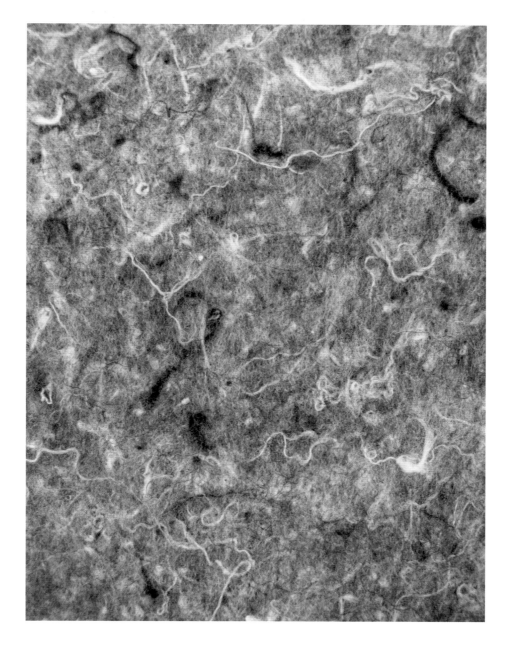

Adobe wall, *Bali.* Traditional adobe walls use straw and other natural materials to help bind clay together, forming a strong wall.

The process of spraying to create a nonwoven is starting to emerge in applications ranging from fashion to geotextiles. The Australian company Spraygrass has developed a spray-on grow mat and seed mat under the brand name EnviroGuard. A specially formulated compound is combined with water and seeds to form a slurry that can then be pumped through a Hydromulcher directly onto the area to be revegetated. The mix then hardens to form a bonded fiber matrix (BFM) in around 24 hours depending on climate conditions. It provides a microclimate for seeds to germinate, with excellent water retention properties and low rainfall runoff. It is especially useful for sloped and irregular areas where conventional rolled or sheet geosynthetics would be difficult to install.

EnviroGuard, *Spraygrass, Australia.* This geotextile both protects and plants seeds in the same spray in an application process that uses fibers as a binding agent. A green paint has been added to show where the ground has been sprayed.

Polyester geomesh,
Maccaferri, UK. The geomesh
has been combined with
a geogrid for additional strength
in applications such as soil
and rock reinforcement.

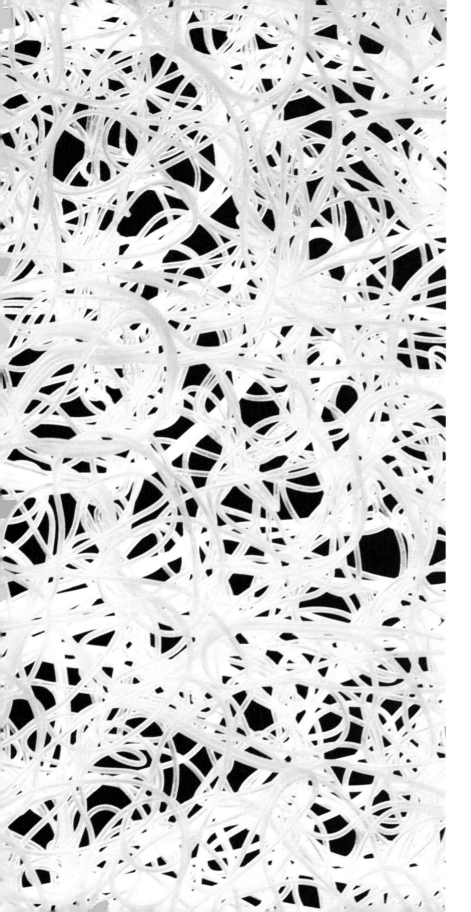

So Flex, *Beco Geosynthetics, Germany*. Entangled three-dimensional mesh structure for comfort and ventilation in furniture applications.

Geosynthetic sandwich structures
combining polyester geogrids and
geomesh with nonwovens. These
are designed for applications in soil
reinforcement and drainage control.

GRIDS AND MESHES

Grids and meshes bear some resemblance to woven and nonwoven structures but differ in that grids are designed to be fixed at the intersection, while meshes are used as long or continuous yarns rather than short-cut fibers. Polypropylene, polyethylene and polyester are all used in these structures. Although adhesives can be used, many employ and ultilize the thermoplastic properties of polyester to heat-bond the grid. Another way of producing the grid is to extrude the material in sheet form before punching or piercing it at regular intervals. The holes can also be made during production as the sheet is being drawn, creating grid apertures. If the sheet is then drawn in a cross-machine direction the apertures are further widened to produce a bi-axially orientated grid. This is particularly useful for applications where stress and structural integrity are required.

Atlanta Nisseki CLAF Inc. (ANCI), a subsidiary of Nippon Petrochemicals Co. Ltd, produce a co-extruded polyethylene fibrillated film under the brand name CLAF. The cross-laminated fabric has a low-profile open mesh construction that can be used to strengthen films, foils and nonwovens for many applications including building and filtration industries. It has a good strength-to-weight ratio so that it adds strength but not bulk or weight to the finished material. It can be further processed with these and other materials as part of the coating and converting process.

SANDWICH STRUCTURES

A sandwich structure is where two or more different materials are placed on top of one another and joined together to form a new single material. The individual structures are usually different and textile and non-textile can be brought together in this way through a variety of joining processes, including heat, stitch and adhesives. Applications vary, ranging from geosynthetics to clothing.

Sandwich structures are very common in the geosynthetics industry where they are used for road and soil reinforcement as well as filtration. Nonwovens are typically combined with a geomesh or grid, with the former performing a filtration function and the latter providing structural reinforcement. Although functionally gradient materials are starting to be developed in earnest, the production of materials to these specifications is still some way off.

The North American company Transhield is producing a layered fabric that can protect fragile goods in transit against corrosion. The system offers a patented vapour corrosion inhibitor (VCI) delivery system to offer protection against corrosion. The outer layer of Transhield is a white polyethylene shrink/stretch film followed by a central layer with an olefin hot melt adhesive, which is solvent free. The inner layer is a soft non-abrasive hydroentangled polyester nonwoven. The covers are made with drawstrings to fit the goods. Once it is fitted, it is manually heated to shrink the fabric so it is a better fit for the boat or other object being

Insul bright, *The Warm Co., USA.* A thin layer of aluminium is sandwiched between two layers of nonwovens to create a lightweight, highly insulating material.

Memory Chairs, *Tokujin Yoshioka Inc., Japan, produced by Moroso.* Sandwich structures combine textile and metal in these chairs so that they can conform to the sitter's shape.

moved or stored. The cover is reusable for a limited period of time.
A very different rationale is used by Tokujin Yoshioka in his Memory Chair
design for the Italian furniture designers Moroso. Cotton and recycled
aluminium are brought together to create a sandwich structure. This
is then formed into a dome shape which is placed over the chair structure
like a sleeve. The user creates the final form to fit their body shape
as the metal can be reformed by sitters to suit their shape and posture.

Stitched carbon fiber prototype.
The technology is aimed at supplying prepregs to be used as the basis for fiber-reinforced composites.

STITCH

Stitch and embroidery are no longer techniques confined to decorative applications. At an industrial level they are capable of very fine work both for large- and small-scale applications. Carbon fiber and electronics for wearable computers or heating systems are among the new developments in this area.

Stitch laying is a process whereby yarns are laid and then stitched into place using either a similar or a different thread. The machines can use carbon and glass fibers as well as aramids and hybrid yarns. A thread is used to stitch the yarns, holding them in place. A computer-aided design (CAD) pattern determines not just the design and finished placement of fibers, but also the sequence of fiber laying. This allows stress points in the finished design to be addressed so that there are no weaknesses or strain where the areas are curved, for instance. Effectively it allows for the creation of a functionally gradient material so that reinforcement can be created where needed and fewer fibers used elsewhere. The base material onto which the fibers are stitched is often a nonwoven, so that the excess can be removed by cutting away or during further processing. It is the fibers that form the performance material with the nonwoven acting as a substrate, sometimes only temporarily.

COMPOSITES

Composites are structures where two or more identifiable materials are brought together to create a new material with enhanced performance characteristics. These are usually three-dimensional and have gained in popularity as energy prices have escalated and concern for environmental impact has grown. The construction and transport industries have been particularly interested in this group of materials, using them as a replacement for heavier materials such as concrete and metal. The structure can be made in a number of ways depending on the intended use.

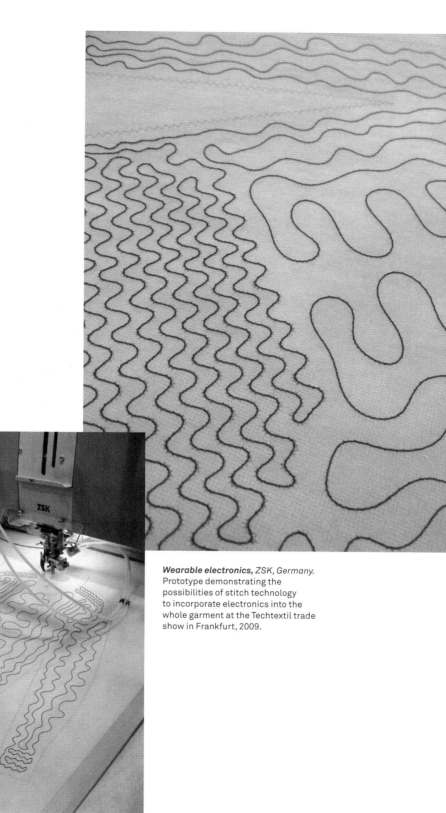

Wearable electronics, ZSK, Germany.
Prototype demonstrating the
possibilities of stitch technology
to incorporate electronics into the
whole garment at the Techtextil trade
show in Frankfurt, 2009.

These pages and overleaf:
Selection of composites,
Design Composite GmbH, Austria.
Colour, translucency and other
aesthetic qualities can be made
to specification as well as the
performance characteristics.

Composites made using a honeycomb-based core structure can vary dramatically in performance depending on the choice of material as well as final construction. Kraft paper, Nomex paper, Kevlar paper and polycarbonate-formed structures are being used. DuPont's Kevlar honeycomb is a typical honeycomb construction: sheets of the aramid paper are layered and bonded together to form panels that are then sliced to the desired thickness. These are then opened out to form the honeycomb structure with the structural force applied to the section cut of the structure. Over 90% of the material is open space, making it super lightweight but strong. It is employed extensively in the aircraft and boat industries.

The Austrian company Design Composite GmbH specialize in the production of translucent and clear composite panels that have applications in architecture, automotive and wind-turbine industries. Their clear-PEP and AIR-board products are translucent with different optical features combined with structural stability making them particularly popular with architects. Polycarbonate is formed into three-dimensional panels with core structures that are honeycomb-

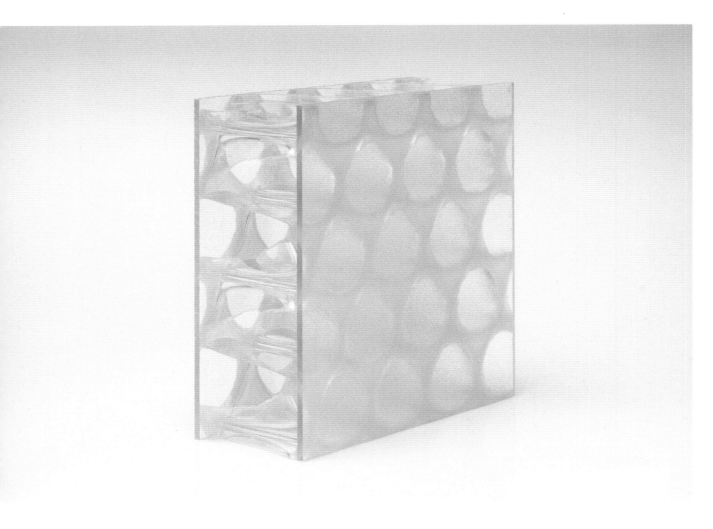

and bamboo-inspired, both having very good strength-to-weight ratios with the ability to let some ambient light through. The open areas within the composite can also be filled for decoration or for additional performance such as acoustic insulation. The versatility of the process in providing light can be seen in two very different collaborations: one with Swarovski and the other with American architects KieranTimberlake Associates LLP.

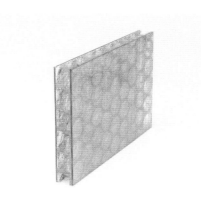

In the project with Swarovski the result is a product entitled Swarovski Honeycomb. A polycarbonate honeycomb structure incorporates up to 33,000 crystals as well as LEDs or fiber optics to specification. Insulated safety glass is used to form a panel on one side and polycarbonate forms a lightweight panel on the other. The product is intended to provide an illuminated wall or ceiling that can be completely customized. KieranTimberlake Associates LLP has used clear-PEP in the design for their Cellophane House. The five-storey dwelling was commissioned by the Museum of Modern Art in New York for their 2008 exhibition *Home Delivery: Fabricating the Modern Dwelling*, which looked at new ways of prefabricating buildings. The Cellophane House takes an environmental approach and looks at how a building might be designed for disassembly. The resulting process is closer to assembly line production in the automotive industry than conventional architecture. The steel frame of the building is bolted together for ease of dismantling and reuse of the various elements, including the clear-PEP used in the floor and ceilings. The composite allows the structure to transmit as much light as possible, while adhering to requirements for environmental safety and stability.

Composites can also be produced using fibers or formed or semi-formed fabric as their basis. Glass and carbon fibers are used where the highest performance is required, with polyester also being employed extensively. Hand lay-up technique is a process whereby the fibers are laid into a mould by hand to the desired thickness. A resin and curing agent are applied to solidify the form which can vary between semi-flexible and fully rigid. Fibers can also be applied by spraying. In addition, flat and three-dimensional fabrics can be used; some are produced semi-formed while others can be shaped, most commonly by heat, forming a thermoplastic material such as polyester. The shaped fabric can then be treated with a resin to achieve the desired strength and rigidity. Alternatively, the textile can be further shaped through processes such as compression moulding, based on the use of metal dyes and the application of hydraulic pressure. These serve to hold the material in place until the resin can be applied and allowed to cure. Resin-transfer moulding and the cold-mould process are also used, particularly for larger components.

The process of filament winding can form the basis for composites. The process sees fibers and yarns employed to create a structure, usually three-dimensional, through the use of a mandrel. This is a long cylindrical tool that is computer controlled and fully automated to place the fibers in a precise manner on a tool as it moves back and forth. The machine is suspended horizontally and generally has between two and twelve axes of motion. The fiber is usually passed through a resin bath just before it reaches the mandrel, in a process

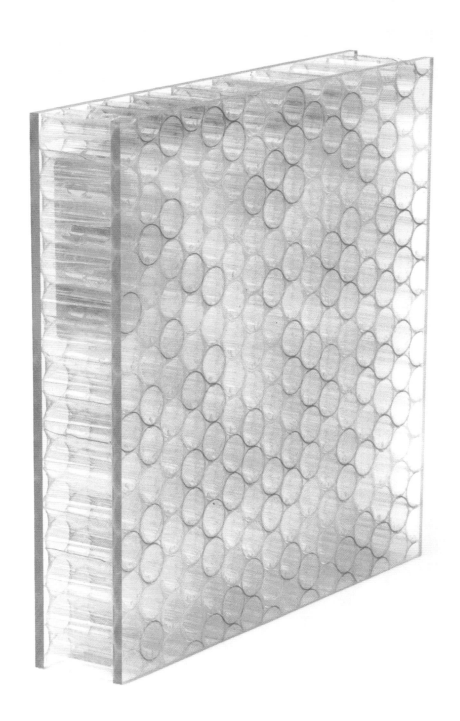

known as wet winding. When the fiber is impregnated with resin it is referred to as a towpreg. Dry winding, as the name suggests, is done without resin but goes on to be used as a preform in another moulding process such as resin transfer moulding (RTM). Very large composite structures such as aircraft fuselages can be undertaken with an automated filament placement (AFP) or an automated tape laying placement (ATP). Both generally involve the use of carbon fiber either as fiber or tape. These can be continuously placed and are designed to meet very stringent strength and rigidity requirements while keeping the weight and material costs to a minimum.

BIOTECHNOLOGY

Biotechnology is the term given to any technological application that uses biological systems – living organisms or their derivatives – to make or modify products or processes for specialist use. The term biotextiles refers to textiles made using biotechnology and is a relatively new area of research and development. It is driven by an interest in engineering nature to provide textiles based on natural materials that have the potential to be very sustainable.

Barkcloth is a technical agroforestry textile that is made from the bark of trees in Uganda without destroying trees in the process. The barkcloth is cultivated from the Mutuba tree, where it is harvested during the rainy season. The material is turned into a soft fabric by beating with hammers, resulting in a unique colour and tactile quality to each sheet while adhering to ISO standards. Oliver Heinz, founder and Managing Director of the European-African family venture Barkcloth, states their objective as 'to show that it is possible to manufacture semi-finished products for industry using manual rather than industrial techniques.' The cloth is treated with different coatings and laminates depending on the intended end use. When coated with latex rubber derived from the sub-bark of the fig tree, the material can be moulded with greater abrasion-, water- and stain-resistant properties. In early 2009 the company began combining the bark with biopolymer resins with the intention of producing a natural fiber laminate that brings together performance and a natural aesthetic. Applications are envisaged in automotive interior, casing and furniture applications. In 2005 barkcloth production was declared by UNESCO to be a cultural heritage of humanity.

The Japanese designer Tokujin Yoshioka has created the material and final form for his collection of crystalline furniture simultaneously. The process starts with moulded skeletons for the chairs made using soft polyester fibers. These are then submerged into a tank containing a mineral solution. Over a period of a month crystals form on the fibers, covering them completely. The designer describes the process as 'half the work is done by me and the other half by nature'. Although the form and process are designed by Yoshioka, there is no way that he can exert complete control over the final outcome. Each piece of furniture is slightly different: though part of a series, each piece is unique, just as no two trees or leaves are exactly the same in nature.

Venus Chair, Tokujin Yoshioka Inc., Japan, 2009. Grown from natural crystals on a textile substrate. The designer attributes half of the production to his design and half to nature.

SURFACE

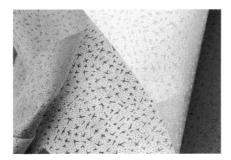

InnovaWipe, *Innovatec, Germany.* Melt-blown nonwoven made from polymer granules. The surface of the microfiber fabric has been embossed with a pattern to increase the liquid absorption and abrasion resistance qualities.

The application of treatments to the surface of the fabric allows for many different and combined functions. The processes include embedding, coating, finishing and applied treatments. They are used to add functional, tactile and aesthetic properties and can even provide the full performance using another base fabric as the substrate or carrier. The materials themselves allow for a wide-ranging mixture of chemical treatments, metals, plastics, yarns and non-textile technologies. Significant advances in this area include nanotechnology and the ability to combine different treatments without reducing their performance.

In most instances the treatment is applied to the surface of the material after construction. There are exceptions, such as embedding, but generally these appear or impact on the surface of the finished textile. With growing concern about the environmental impact of all textiles, there is a noticeable move towards reducing the number of processes, many of which have to be undertaken in different locations with the associated increase in carbon footprint. Incorporating the surface treatment at an earlier stage in production, even during the construction process, is an issue about which manufacturers are becoming more mindful. The growing number of coated yarns is also indicative of this trend. However, it is unlikely that it will ever be possible or desirable to integrate these processes fully into the fabric construction process. As technologies continue to be refined and new processes developed, the fabric surface looks set to continue as a key area of innovation.

EMBEDDING

The process of embedding chemicals within the fabric has many benefits, as it can allow a more comprehensive application of the treatment so that it does not simply sit on the surface. Techniques used include microencapsulation and melt spinning. Microencapsulation incorporates chemicals such as phase change materials (PCM) used by Schoeller Textiles AG and other manufacturers. The PCM changes state depending on the temperature, going from a solid to a liquid in a process that is also reversible. The chemicals were originally recognized by NASA for applications in the space industry, but are now used in fabric applications such as clothes for motorcyclists and sportswear as well as intimate apparel to protect the wearer from extreme temperatures.

Phase Change Material (PCM), *Schoeller Textiles AG, Switzerland.* The PCM treatment is used to keep the body at a comfortable temperature and can be applied to a range of fabrics including fleece.

The American textile manufacturer AccuMED Innovative Technologies produces custom products for a range of industries including medical and sportswear. Their SILVERtec fabric is a composite that provides breathability and anti-bacterial qualities and is intended primarily for the medical products market. This is an area where devices such as orthopaedic braces or respiratory headgear have to be worn throughout the day or during the night. Breathe-O-Prene uses an open-cell construction to perform a wicking function, moving moisture away from the body and allowing it to evaporate on the surface of the fabric. This leaves the body cool, dry and more comfortable. The addition of embedded silver ensures an active bacteria barrier that lasts for up to 30 washes. The silver chloride (AgCl) nanocrystals are embedded into the Breathe-O-Prene fabric. Colourless, odourless and non-abrasive, they are designed to be used for wound care and burn victims as well as in sporting goods.

The Belgian bespoke tailor Scabal incorporates gold and diamonds into their cloths. These are primarily for their luxury and aesthetic value. Their use of lapis lazuli brings a lustre to the cloth, but is also held to carry therapeutic qualities that are both physical and spiritual. It is considered to be beneficial to the immune system as well as enhancing the wearer's clarity of mind. The finely ground stone is evenly distributed by hand at the end of the weaving process. Combined with a fine wool, the cloth is further enhanced with a paper-press finish and comes in a range of 14 designs.

Aimed at a very different market sector, TexOLED is a German government-funded initiative comprised of a group of research institutes looking at ways of incorporating lighting into textiles. Each institute takes a different approach, with Fraunhofer IZM focusing on the integration of bare-die LEDs into fabrics. The institute is using a conductive bonding process to apply the LEDs. The lights are first cut from their wafer and used without their housing so that the bare LEDs are contacted to the fabric with a machine-jetted isotropic conductive adhesive. The adhesive is jetted onto the fabric at right angles close to the LED. As it touches the fabric it flattens, making it connect with the electrode of the small light while simultaneously contacting the conductor in the fabric. The high viscosity keeps the adhesive in place until it is cured.

Lapis Lazuli, Scabal, Belgium. The semi-precious stone incorporated into the wool fabric is believed to have a beneficial effect on the immune system. The stone itself is used in alternative therapies to counteract throat infections and heal spinal cord injuries.

PRINTING

Since the introduction of digital printing for textiles, researchers have been looking for better and more exciting inks and considering what other materials might be digitally printed. One area of development has been the printing of electronic circuits onto textiles for use in wearable technology. The benefits include flexibility, comfort, weight- and bulk-reduction as well as a more robust system than conventionally applied electronics. In Canada, Xerox scientists have developed Silver Bullet, a silver ink that can be printed onto a variety of substrates including textiles as a replacement for silicon circuits. Three components are used to create integrated circuits – a semi-conductor, a conductor and a dielectric element. Traditionally manufactured in silicon chip fabricating factories, it is an expensive process. In this new process Xerox has developed all three of the materials necessary for printing plastic circuits in a continuous feed. The nanoscale silver dots used in the process offer the potential for much lower-cost production with possible applications in wearable electronics, wearable sensors and radio frequency identification (RFID) tags.

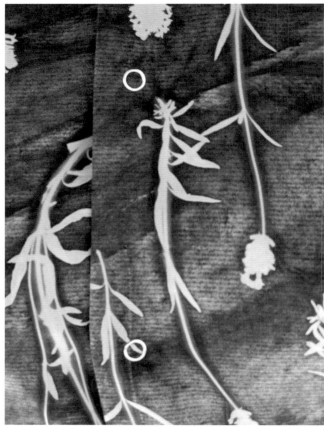

Radiotherapy treatment gowns,
Rebecca Earley, UK, 1999. These hospital gowns for cancer patients were commissioned by the Queen Elizabeth Centre for the Treatment of Cancer, Public Art Commissions Agency. They were designed and printed using a photogram process where the plants are printed directly onto fabric. The imagery shows homeopathic plants used in the care of cancer patients; the plants vary according to the type of cancer.

The Methode Development Co. has developed an ink that contains conductive silver nanoparticles for inkjet printing electrical circuits directly onto treated polyesters. The process allows engineers to go from desktop to prototype and manufacturing without the need for additional curing or processing. The conductive ink uses a thermal inkjet desktop printer with the same print head as that used for industrial print systems, making the move from sampling and prototyping to production relatively easy. Looking to applications in the medical and healthcare industries, Toumaz Technology Ltd is developing Sensium, a digital plaster. The intention is to allow patients greater ease of movement while in hospital and to have their health monitored from home so that they can be discharged from hospital earlier. The low-power disposable plaster incorporates a reconfigurable sensor interface, a digital block with a processor and an RF transceiver block. Along with an external sensor, the device allows doctors to monitor ECG, temperature, blood glucose and oxygen levels.

Gorscuba print, *Maharishi, UK, 2001.*
This urban streetstyle Fu Splinter
camouflage pattern has been printed
with a reflective ink so it appears grey
until the artificial light catches and
illuminates it. The design is also used
on clothing.

Reflective print, 3M, USA. Sampler showing range of coloured reflective inks produced by the company. In daylight each appears as a colour, but at night, under artificial light, they illuminate as a 'white' light.

Schoeller Spirit with glow in the dark, Schoeller Textiles AG, Switzerland, 2011. Lightweight fabric from Spirit range with a glow in the dark check print on the reverse.

Shape innovations hologram, Schoeller Textiles AG, Switzerland, 2011. Lightweight non-elastic fabric with shape memory effect and a facetted hologram coating to dazzle and reflect light; it is used in apparel.

It can also interface pressure and temperature sensors. The 3Plast is a European Commission funded research project looking at the development of printable, pyroelectrical and piezoelectrical large-area sensor technology. One of the areas that they are looking at is printing onto flexible substrates to create more user-friendly sensors, particularly for healthcare. Polymer sensors are combined with organic electronics to provide accurate information on changes in pressure and temperature. Dr Stephanie P. Lacour and the Stretchable BioElectronics Group at the University of Cambridge, England are also investigating the possibilities of stretchability in an electronic system with applications in areas such as textiles and artificial skin, where the system could create a soft biointerface. The group is developing electronics that can be shaped and stretched, and are biocompatable. The researchers have found that an elastomeric material with a fine gold film can be stretched and relaxed with the metal forming a percolating network. This structure allows the metal to twist and deflect without failure as the fabric is stretched. The stretchable gold conductors can be patterned by the process of shadow masking or photolithography. The same process is being used by the researchers to create stretchable touch sensors using a silicone rubber. These are capable of registering strain, pressure and even highly sensitive finger touch.

A number of companies are producing printed photovoltaic cells using inkjet printing-related processes. The importance of these technologies is that they are producing smaller and more flexible panels that move towards a scale and weight that makes them more suitable for applications in wearable clothing. In America, Nanosolar use a copper indium gallium diselenide (CIGS) technology, while in the UK, G24 Innovations use a form of reel-to-reel process to make its dye-sensitized solar cells (DSSC). The dye-sensitized solar cells have been compared with photosynthesis in nature. As sunlight falls on the solar cells it is absorbed by the dye, causing a transfer of electrons as they are released by a redox reaction.

The Technical University of Denmark's (DTU) Riso National Laboratory for Sustainable Energy is looking to the future of solar power, one that is based on the use of flexible polymer solar cells. These are currently far less efficient than single crystalline solar cells, but the initiative is aimed at getting designers and manufacturers to plan for future efficiencies that will see a more widespread use of the technology. In a collaboration with students at Designskole in Copenhagen, they have developed a textile-based printed solar panel that can be used in fashion. Students Tine Hertz and Maria Langberg from Designskole have worked with the lab to create a manufacturing process that is based on silkscreen printing. The photovoltaic printed fabrics can be sewn together to form garments and create three-dimensional forms.

COATINGS

The ability to produce increasingly fine coatings with minimal impact on the material below is resulting in the use of performance chemicals on man-made, natural and technonatural fabrics. The Swiss manufacturer Schoeller Textiles AG has developed Liquid Shell, which, when applied to leather, offers improved resistance to abrasion, and UV-A and UV-B rays, and good resistance to acid and alkaline sweat without a noticeable loss in handle or aesthetic. It makes the material more suitable for extreme sports and marine applications, areas it had not been widely used in before. Looking to recycling, the Taiwanese manufacturer Jeen Wei Enterprise Co. Ltd is making 100% PET as well as fabrics that offer a combination of recycled PET and polyester as the basis for a range of coating treatments which give UV protection, and are waterproof, breathable, anti-bacterial and flame-retardant.

The use of silver for anti-bacterial purposes can be traced back to the writings of Hippocrates with more recent uses in modern medicine for the treatment of burn victims. The technology is now being used for anti-microbial textiles using a variety of processes including flocking. Flock fibers are those that have been cut short, typically between 0.3 and 5 mm in length. They can be made of viscose, polyester, polyamide, polyacryl and polypropylene. The fabric substrate is coated with an adhesive and the flocking applied.

Oriental flower chair, Helen Amy Murray, UK, 2008. The chair uses Cool System black leather which retains 66% less heat than untreated dark leather. Murray has also used a Flashlite retro-reflective fabric from IBR S.r.l. in the appliqué.

Performance coated fabrics,
Schoeller Textiles AG, Switzerland.
A range of high-performance fabrics
from the Swiss company, which
combines fibers and metals in the
weave or coatings with additional
performance treatments brought
together according to the customer's
requirements. These can include a
c-change climate control membrane,
Active Silver to control bacteria,
and nanosphere for self-cleaning
characteristics.

Key application areas include the automotive and packaging industries.
There is an increasing demand for anti-bacterial properties in textiles,
and flocked fabrics are no exception. Testing conducted at the University
of Jena in Germany indicates that flock inserted with a finely ground ion
exchanger allows for the bonding of substantial quantities of silver.

Schoeller Textiles AG were one of the first to bring a nanocoated textile
to the market with their nanosphere coating technology. The engineering
of this ultra-fine water-repellent coating was inspired by the lotus
leaf, which has a bumpy surface texture and wax-like finish to repel
water, the runoff taking dust and other dirt with it. The company refer
to its performance as a 'self-cleaning effect' in which water, dirt and
oil are repelled. Because of this function, nanosphere-coated fabrics
require less frequent and lower temperature washing, an environmental
consideration that is growing in importance.

Silicone rubber is a unique synthetic that is made from a cross-linked polymer that has been reinforced with silica. Used as a coating on technical textiles, it can provide the benefit of being water-, UV- and chemical-resistant and can be flame-retardant. It can also function at temperatures as low as -85°C (-121°F). It can be applied using various processes including dip or immersion coating, spraying, extrusion and rotogravure coating. It is used on both natural and synthetic materials to improve functionality or to modify the appearance and tactility. The American company Dow Corning is producing a silicone rubber impact protection system under the brand name Active Protection System (APS). To enhance the protection and comfort of garments, the technology absorbs and dissipates impact energy to reduce the amount of force felt by the wearer. The benefit of this over harder systems, which can involve rigid textiles or metal-plate inserts, is that it allows greater ease of movement and thermal control. There are two products in

Deflexion S-Range textile, Dow Corning, USA. This three-dimensional knitted spacer fabric has been combined with silicone rubber to absorb and dissipate energy on impact while remaining breathable. Applications for this material are in protective clothing.

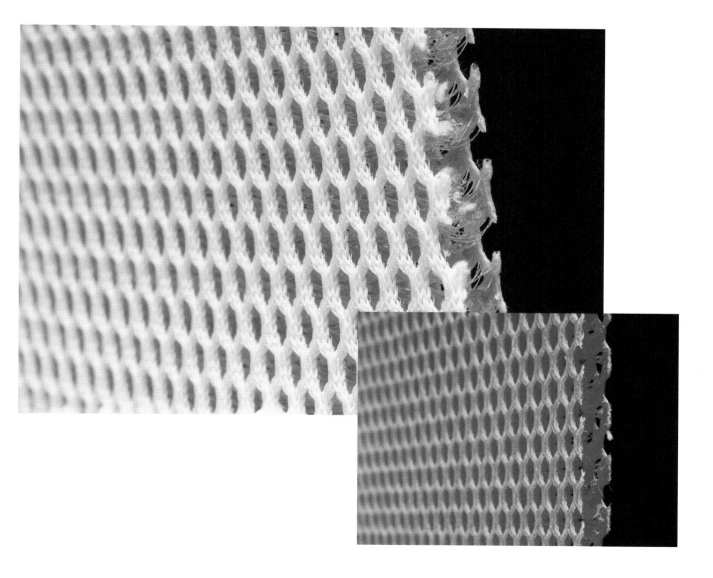

Opposite and overleaf: **Nanosphere coating**, *Schoeller Textiles AG, Switzerland*. Dynatec Power Stretch fabric coated with a nanosphere stain- and water-resistant coating. The nanotechnology is inspired by the textured surface of the lotus leaf in nature, which reduces the contact point on the surface, making it difficult for dirt and water to stick.

this range: the S-Range and the TP-Range. The S-Range is based on three-dimensional spacer fabrics that are impregnated with the silicones. Spacer fabrics are inherently good on breathability and can be produced in a wide range of densities and thicknesses. Thermoplastic silicones form the basis for the TP-Range which can be supplied in the form of flat sheets or rolls. It is also possible to produce both with perforations. Patterns are cut from the sheet and these can then be thermoformed to create three-dimensional shapes without seams. The forms can be inserted into pouches on garments or glued directly onto a fabric.

There are a number of flame-retardant coatings that are commonly used and some new developments are appearing on the market. The Belgian company Nanocyl specialize in nanotechnologies (discussed in more detail in Chapter 1), which include flame-retardant coatings for textiles. Thermocyl incorporates carbon nanotubes engineered specially for this application in a thermoset matrix. In addition to its main protective function, it can also offer high thermal conductivity, anti-fouling, release properties and, under certain conditions, anti-static.

FINISHES

Finishing treatments offer protection to the fabrics themselves as well as to humans, improving their wear and often reducing the need for cleaning. Manufacturers are increasingly looking to reassess the environmental impact of the chemicals they use as part of a greater awareness and concern for the environment.

The Swiss company Clariant International Ltd specializes in chemicals for textile finishes and dyestuffs. They have developed a range of Nuva N series fluorocarbons based on C6 chemistry that is free of perfluorooctanoic acid (PFOA) following concern that PFOA may be carcinogenic and thus harmful with prolonged exposure. Nuva N is oil- and water-repellent and is used in treatments for textiles employed in architecture, medicine and transport. The Appretan N5122 liq and N5127 liq chemicals are used in the building industry for heat sealing and lamination. They are soil- and dirt-repellent and offer high abrasion resistance. The Nuva N2116 liq is used in the nonwovens industry for medical applications to provide a clean and hygienic surface for the textiles. The Appretan E4959 liq performs a similar function in the automotive industry, where it is used in needle-punched carpets, pleated filters and roof linings.

In some applications, such as biogas holders, a waterproof coating is the starting point for a long list of requirements. In India, SRF Ltd is producing a PVC-coated fabric for use in biogas holders as well as SRF effluent treatment plant membranes which need to have a finish that is not only waterproof, but also flame-retardant, fungus- and termite-resistant, impermeable to gases and stable in the presence of methane. The company sees methane as a potential source of low-cost renewable energy, particularly in countries such as India with a large agriculture economy where cattle feature prominently. In urban areas, canteen and municipal waste can also be used to generate methane.

LAMINATES

Lamination is the process by which two or more materials are united using a bonding material. This is usually performed using heat and pressure, but it can also involve light-activated adhesives, moisture, or a combination of these. A flat-bed vacuum laminator or roll-to-roll laminator may be used as a surface treatment to the fabric or as a way of producing a new material.

Gore medical fabrics use lamination as a surface treatment, producing a membrane that is impervious to liquids but remains breathable because its microscopic pores allow for 1.4 billion pores per centimetre. This is about 20,000 times smaller than a drop of water. Gore Comfortable Liquid Proof Fabric (CLIP) is an expanded polytetrafluoroethylene (ePTFE). The membrane is laminated to the fabric substrate so that it is permanently adhered to the surface, or in some instances between two layers of material, commonly polyester. It provides protection against liquids, micro-organisms and viruses as well as enhanced comfort; the fabric is designed primarily for use in surgeon's gowns. It has good tactile qualities and can be sterilized using steam. Gore Liquid Proof Drape Fabrics is a similar product for the patient market, in a heavier weight and with greater liquid absorption properties.

The medical and healthcare market is also behind the development of stretchable circuit boards (SCB) which are currently being developed by Fraunhofer IZM as part of the European Union funded project STELLA (stretchable electronics for large area applications). In one of their developments (a collaboration with TU Berlin), an elastic thermoplastic polyurethane (TPU) foil acts as a substrate. The conductive copper wires applied to the fabric are inherently rigid. In order to make them flexible, the wires have been structured into the substrate in a series of tiny meandering patterns. This allows stretch capacity of up to 300%. A priority from the outset of the project has been to maintain a conventional circuit-board manufacturing process. To achieve this a thick copper film is laminated onto the TPU which is then structured using conventional lithography or etching methods. The stretchable circuit board is integrated into the textile using a standard heat press, doing so in a way that allows the electronics to be adhered to the material. Anticipated applications for the development include those where sensors have to be worn close to the body to measure vital signs. A new product suggested by the technology and being developed by project partners under STELLA is a baby jersey to monitor breathing. This is seen as something that could help in the prevention of Sudden Infant Death Syndrome (SIDS). Other developments being researched include an intelligent bandage to detect whether it is too tight or to check for secretions, and a plaster to accelerate wound healing by applying electrostimulation.

Trans-Textil GmbH are producing laminate finishes with the aim of improving environmental credentials alongside performance. They are approaching this in a number of different ways. Topaz Airtouch has an aqueous base so that additional benefits can be incorporated as it is applied in fine droplets to a membrane. This helps to protect the membrane from wear while making it light and pleasant to wear next to the skin, thus eliminating the need for a lining on the garment. Topaz Dual

Geogrid, *Synteen, USA*. Polyester geogrid with PVC coating and high visibility colour to enable it to be easily seen in poor conditions.

Guard provides a double performance for fabrics: it repels water, oil and dirt and offers improved, easier removal of oil and other stains. Used on high visibility clothing, it improves their functionality and performance. The Topaz Bi-micro membrane combines the characteristics of a microporous ePTFE membrane with a layer of microporous protective polymer coating. Cocona, the activated carbon derived from coconut husks, can also be incorporated. These thin, yet high-performance, finishes are predominantly aimed at protective, sports and leisurewear.

The German manufacturer Recytex is using recycled textiles in their product range. In the 1990s they worked on the Tandem closed recycling concept for the use of textiles in automotive interiors with various partners, including Mercedes-Benz AG. The company take textile waste from different stages in the production process and rework it into a nonwoven to be used instead of polyurethane foam. Many of their materials are subject to further treatments, notably lamination to enhance and add properties. RECYcombi combats vibration and noise. It must also be resistant to rotting fuel spills and have good aesthetic qualities. The resulting laminate begins with a self-adhesive film, which

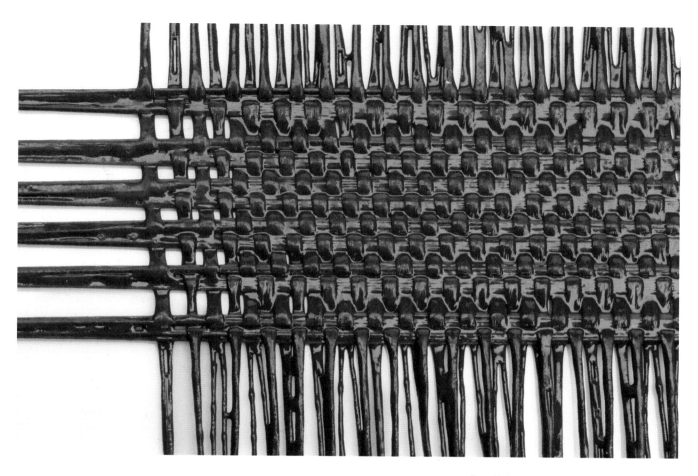

Geogrid, *Synteen, USA*. Green polyester geogrid with PVC coating to strengthen it for applications in ground reinforcement.

is followed by fleece and then a heavy toil layer. A thick layer of fleece then comes before a quilted structured surface material comprised of a glass fiber and finally an aluminized layer. In a variation on the structure, RECYtherm uses a self-adhesive film, then the fleece and finally a PE film with an aluminium cover for heat and sound applications in building interiors.

The demands of protective garments often place very high requirements on the performance of fabrics over their lifetime. Kleibert's PUR hot melt system of lamination means that the strength of the bond is only reached on the cooling of the adhesive coupled with a chemical cross linking. This provides good thermal and chemical resistance as well as good wear and wash test results. The Czech company Tebo laminate using a process of hot-melt adhesive foils, mesh and fleece. The foils can be ethylene vinyl acetate (EVA)-based, copolyamide, copolyester or polyurethane. The process sees the fabric built up in layers as each one is passed through heat then through roller compression before having the temperature reduced once again during a procedure that fixes the laminate to stabilize. Additional properties of fireproofing, water repellency and anti-bacterial treatments can be added to many of the company's textiles.

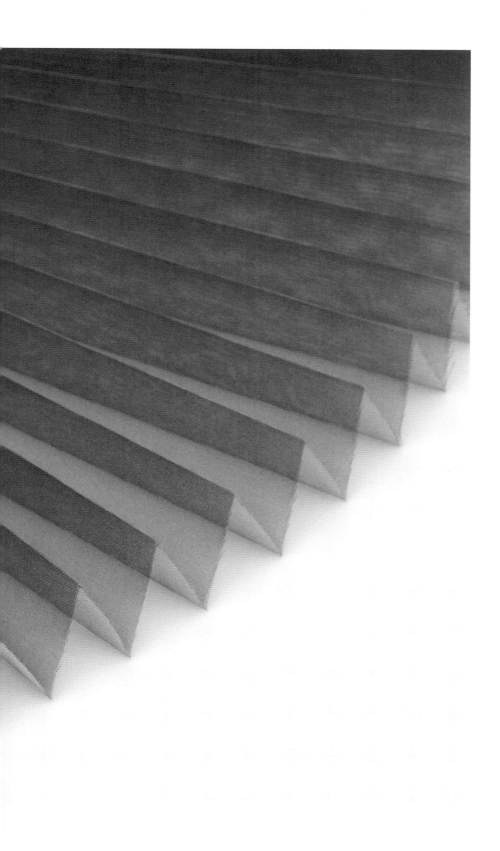

Metalized Trevira CS, *Verosol, The Netherlands*. This aluminized fabric provides protection from the sun and is available pleated and flat for use in blinds and curtains. It can be produced in varying degrees of transparency (5–41%) and is capable of 74% reflection. It is treated with a flame-retardant coating.

Sail technology can play a significant role in determining the winners and losers of races such as the America's Cup and the challenging Sydney Hobart Yacht Race which takes place in some of the most difficult waters of the world. The Australia company Aeronaut produce special machines, including an extra wide span carbon fiber gantry machine. This measures 10.5 m (34½ ft) in width, making it ideal for large sailcloths. Commonly referred to as a 'stringer', the machine is linked to a computerized design programme that allows fiber orientation and laying to be done in a completely automated way. The laminate substrate is treated with a special laminate adhesive so that the fibers stick to the base film on impact and are then further reinforced with the addition of a subsequent layer of laminate film before being cured.

'Stringer' sail technology,
Aeronaut Automation Pty Ltd,
Australia. The aramid fibers are
seen being precision laid, before
a very high temperature is applied,
with the final image showing a
detail of the yarn structure within
the laminate.

The Aeronaut technology is used by Dimension-Polyant GmbH in the D4 and D4 Multi Panel systems of their sailcloths. The company's D4 process uses a wide range of films and taffetas, or woven fabrics, as well as high-performance fibers such as carbon fibers, aramids and Vectran. This is a high-end bespoke product where the exact layout of each fiber is computer designed to calculate load paths before the fiber is laid on the laminate. The fibers are machine laid onto a laminate that has been coated with an adhesive before a further laminate or combination of laminate and taffeta-woven fabric is placed on top. The resins and aramid fibers are treated with UV inhibitors and anti-microbial additives help to maximize the lifespan of the sailcloth. Taffetas are treated with a surface coating of titanium dioxide as well as the anti-microbial agent for protection against UV and mildew.

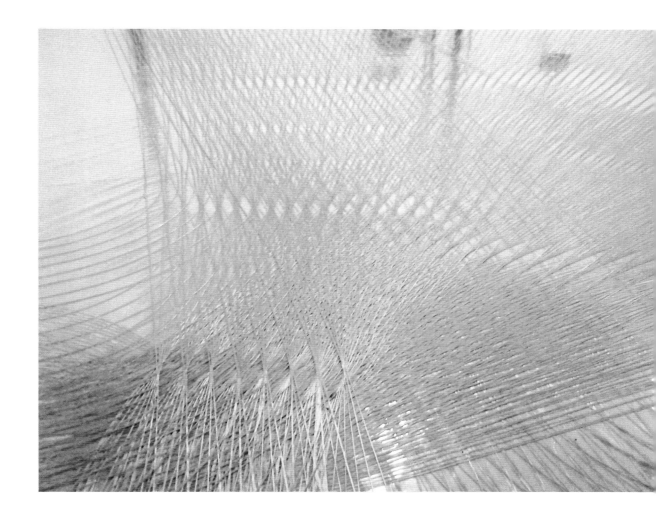

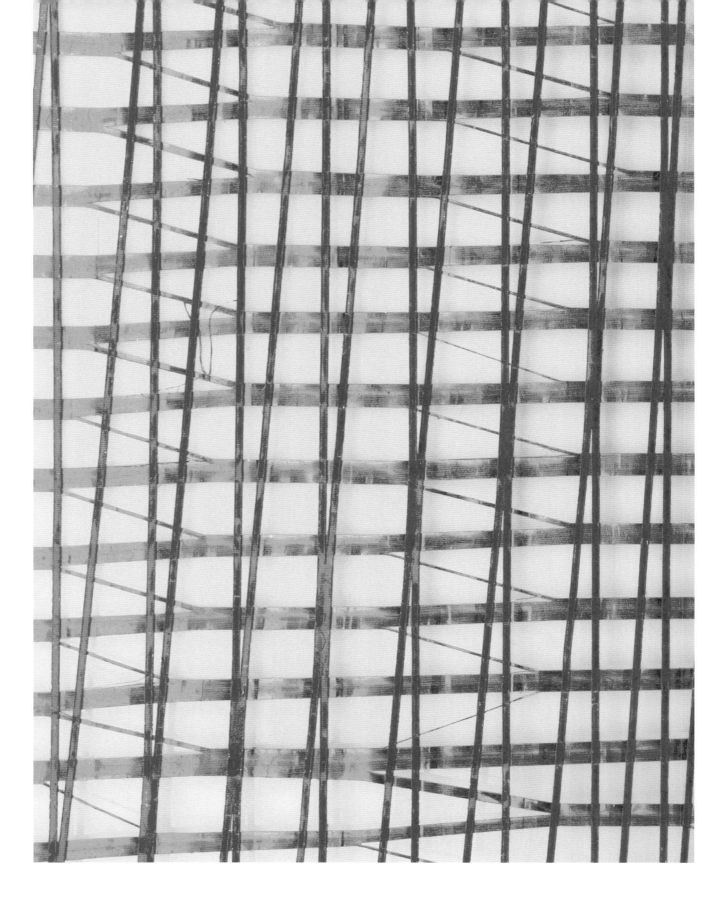

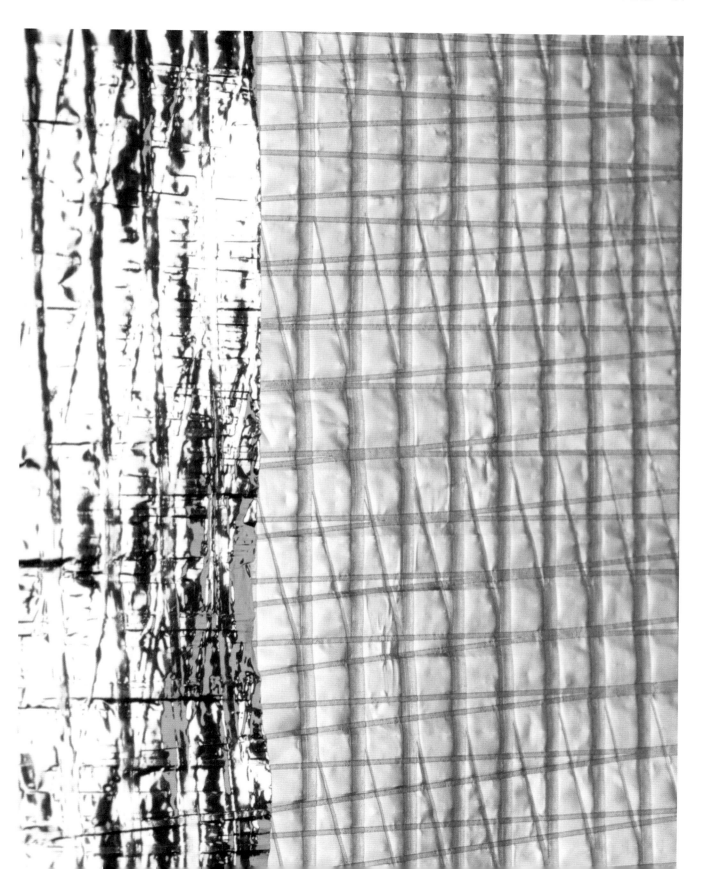

Left and previous pages:
Laminated sailcloths, *Dimension-Polyant GmbH, Germany*. As ocean conditions vary, the yarns and laminates can be custom made to be responsive to the changing climate, offering low or relatively high flex as required.

Dimension-Polyant GmbH specializes in sailcoths that utilize laminate technologies. The company has developed a range of sailcloths focusing on the weave and laminate. Dimension-Polyant's Hydra Net uses a Dyneema/polyester fabric. Because of the high strength of the polyethylene Dyneema, and the very tight weave, the sails can be given very good shape retention along with soft tactile qualities, which works particularly well with low-stretch sails. The GraphX range of carbon laminates incorporates high-strength carbon warp sheet fiber with a Technora (para-aramid) Black base and Technora Black X-Ply (X-patterned woven fabric created by the use of continuous inserted yarn). The result is a fabric that is extremely strong and resistant to elongation and UV degradation. Each side of the textile is covered with a laminate film and sandwiched between these is a diamond-shaped net of X-Ply, then a Technora Black scrim and finally carbon fiber inserts. The woven fabrics have been produced on wide-width looms and designed to produce flat, straight fabrics for minimum bulk within the laminate. Where performance requirements are lower, the company's CXT low-stretch durable laminates use a light polyester taffeta on both sides with an internal scrim also of polyester that holds the shape and prevents the sail from tearing in high winds.

HABITAT

Technologies such as air conditioning and central heating have transformed how our buildings look and behave. These advances have undoubtedly led to more pleasant and comfortable buildings to live in, but at an environmental cost. Although our cities are no longer blackened by coal soot from the chimneys, the energy needed to run the new technologies is causing a more devastating effect on our ecosystem. Textiles are forming part of the solution to making our buildings better places to live in the present and for future generations.

Textiles are once again being used as the basis for whole structures, often as lightweight and easily transportable shelter. Regulating temperature within buildings and providing protection from solar glare are other areas where advanced textiles are providing solutions. They are being applied to existing buildings and created for new ones to reduce energy consumption. The further wellbeing of the occupants is being addressed through control fabrics that address noise, fire hazard and air pollution. One of the notable achievements of these materials is that they are much more design led and visible to the architect and occupant. This serves to highlight their presence and function and our own consumption.

Tropical Islands Resort, *SIAT, Germany, 2000.* This Tropical Islands Resort has been converted into an indoor resort which can accommodate up to 8,000 people with a Birdair PVC-coated polyester membrane and liner that allows it to maintain a comfortable climate all year.

The National Aquatics Centre, *PTW Architects, Engineers: Arup, Beijing, 2008* (interior view, overleaf). Most commonly referred to as the Water Cube, the use of Vector Foiltec's ETFE cushions has allowed for a building design that would not be possible in any other building material. The interior view shows the quality of light that permeates through the ETFE cushions. Arup provided the structural engineering and the design was inspired by the random forms of soap bubbles.

Dedmon Athletic Center,
Birdair, Radford, Virginia, 2009.
The centre uses Transtherm
membrane with aerogel to provide
thermal insulation and moisture
control while maximizing the daylight
coming into the building.

THERMAL

The issue of thermal control in buildings is of primary concern to
architects and engineers alike. The challenge is how to insulate in
a way that allows for the most efficient energy use during the lifetime
of the building. This is coupled with a desire that it should be easy to
install, sometimes retrospectively, and not impact on the aesthetics
of the architecture. Conventionally, insulation is incorporated into
the roofing, walls and flooring, out of sight. However, the popularity
of architectural membrane roofing has caused textile manufacturers
to think again about how these properties might be incorporated into
textiles that are visible to the public gaze.

The use of ethylene tetrafluoroethylene (ETFE) foils is becoming more
common. ETFE is a polymer that can offer thermal and acoustic control
as well as shade when printed on. It is capable of expanding to three times
its normal length without loss of elasticity, which makes it ideal for use
in inflatable pillow-like structures. At around 1% of the weight of glass,
it is an important alternative for large-scale structures. Vector Foiltec
is the company behind much of the research and development of the
material for the construction industry and have supplied fabric for many
of the most innovative buildings in this area.

The National Aquatics Centre has become one of the most iconic buildings
that marked the 2008 Beijing Olympic Games. Commonly known as
the Water Cube, the centre was designed by China State Construction
Engineering Corporation (CSCEC) and Australian architects Peddle Thorpe

Walker (PTW) with architectural engineers Arup. The structure houses five swimming pools as well as a restaurant and has seating capacity for 17,000 spectators. ETFE forms the basis for the building's aesthetic alongside its protective function. Vector Foiltec's Texlon ETFE pneumatic cushions have been used in the construction. These are inflated with low-pressure air in order to provide thermal insulation, capturing as much as 20% of the solar energy that can then be utilized for heating. The building is also mindful of a water shortage in the city and is designed to reuse and recycle 80% of the water collected from its roof and other areas.

Birdair has worked with the Cabot Corporation to combine a translucent architectural membrane with a highly insulating aerogel. The result is transtherm glass fiber with nanogel. Aerogel is the world's most effective and lightest solid thermal insulation. Its insulating properties do not deteriorate over time and under compression the aerogel insulating value increases whereas most insulations lose some of their insulating performance. Because it is a hydrophobic material, nanogel cannot hold or be affected by moisture, making it ideal for applications in architectural membranes. The aerogel is sandwiched between two layers of polytetrafluoroethylene (PTFE)-coated fiberglass, reducing

The Sony Centre, *Murphy Jahn Inc. Architects, Berlin, 1999.* Forty-eight individual Birdair PTFE membrane panels are needed to cover around 5,300 sq m (57,000 sq ft) of surface area in this open-air structure. The use of the membrane protects against the weather without losing too much daylight.

heating, ventilating and air conditioning (HVAC) energy consumption and costs. The membrane has been used in the Dedmon Athletic Center, Radford, Virginia with the expectation that it will quadruple the roof's thermal insulation performance without losing any of the original roof's translucency. The material also allows the 4,830 sq m (52,000 sq ft) facility to incorporate air conditioning, something which had not been possible in the past. Nanogel itself has been awarded a Cradle to Cradle Silver certification from McDonough Braungart Design Chemistry (MBDC).

Enric Ruiz-Geli's 'Thirst Pavilion' for the Expo 2008 in Zaragoza, Spain, also used ETFE. The temporary structure was designed to offer thermal control through an active façade that could sweat. No air conditioning was used and instead the Buckminster Fuller-inspired domed structure incorporated temperature monitors allowing the internal climate to be altered to maintain a comfortable ambient environment. The skin used three layers of ETFE with a layer of fiberglass sandwiched in between. Operating on the same principles as human perspiration, the fabric sends salt water to the surface of the building when heated by the sun. The water evaporates in the outdoor heat, which leaves the salt to crystallize, so building up layers over time to form what the architect refers to as an igloo of salt. When it rains, the salt is dissolved and returned to the system and the process then begins once more.

ACOUSTIC

While there is a high awareness of pollution in outdoor environments, particularly urban and industrial, the question of air quality in buildings is not so well recognized. Textile-based filtration systems are becoming standard in high-rise buildings where it is not possible to open windows to let stale air out and fresh air in, so that the air is controlled by air conditioning units. Higher density living and thinner partitioning walls, floors and ceilings mean that sound insulation has become a high priority in building design. Conventionally, these, largely nonwoven, fabrics were placed out of sight behind cladding. There is a growing trend, however, to make them more visible as the possibility for creating three-dimensional acoustic control fabrics has become both a technical and economic possibility. Architects and designers are embracing the potential of this technology to allow for a new aesthetic as well as a technical solution to sound control within enclosed spaces. In the Netherlands, Bakers Architects has worked with

Court de Brug, Amsterdam, *Bakers Architects, 2009.* Driessen + van Deijne has designed a series of artworks which combine aesthetics with sound absorption and flame retardancy using a Tempo Trevira CS fabric.

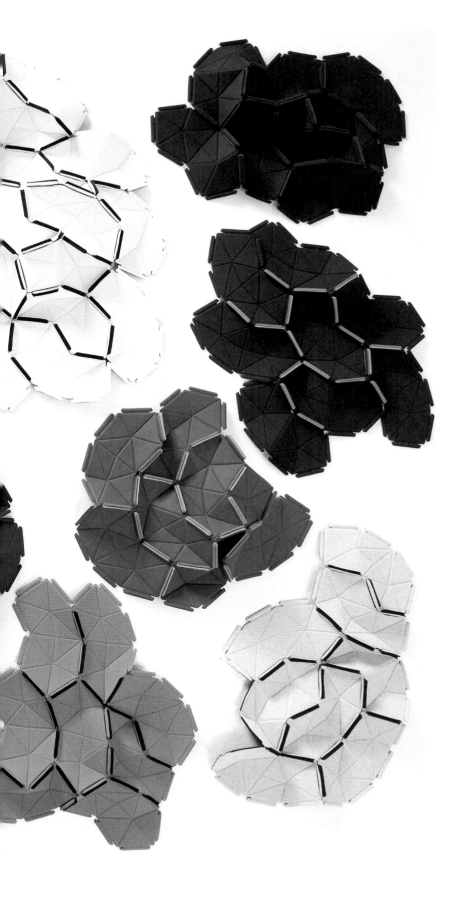

***Clouds**, Ronan and Erwan Bouroullec
for Kvadrat.* Interlocking acoustic fabric
tiles that can be hung from the ceiling
or on the wall or floor. Available in
Divina (wool) or Tempo (Trevira CS)
fabrics, different colour combinations
make this a playful alternative to
conventional acoustic insulation.

Opposite and overleaf: *Acoustic fabric concrete, The Tactility Factory, UK.* These prototypes are part of an ongoing investigation into the combination of aesthetic, sustainable and acoustic performance characteristics that textiles can bring to concrete. Textile structures, including lace and knit, are included as well as different finishing treatments such as flock and gold leaf.

Driessen + van Deijne to create a textile-based art intervention for the corridor walls of the Court of Amsterdam de Brug. Acoustic insulation was a technical requirement of the work, as was flame retardancy. The result is a layered system, with a nonwoven fabric providing sound insulation sandwiched behind a digitally printed Trevira CS fabric that provided flame retardancy as well as the aesthetic qualities. The design is based on the drape, movement and layering of textiles. These were first photographed and then digitally altered to create a series of soft images defined by subtle colours. The alteration of scale abstracts the original source of the images, creating a diffuse installation that contrasts with the harder materials in the corridor space.

In her product currently under development entitled QWaiet Double, Margareta Zetterblom is developing smart wool that will allow the material to sense and respond to changing noise levels, so providing optimum noise control. The researcher is part of the Smart Textiles unit at the Swedish School of Textiles in Boras and is also collaborating with Acqwool Development in the development of the acoustic wool panels. Felted wool forms are the basis for the research. Ribbed on both sides, they absorb sound effectively and also provide thermal insulation. Embedded microphones are intended to pick up sound and, at a certain level, a series of integrated shape memory metal wires will be activated to change shape through the application of electricity to channeled conductive yarns. The material will change shape into a more effective form to absorb sound. There are many challenges to resolving this product. The smart materials themselves and the wool have to be just the right density. If the felting leaves the structure too open then it is not effective, but if it is too tightly compact then no sound can be absorbed.

Patricia Belford and Ruth Morrow have combined to form the Tactility Factory, working at Interface: Centre for Research in Art, Technologies and Design which is part of the University of Ulster in Belfast. Their aim is to create an acoustic and tactile concrete that incorporates fabrics. The textile element operates on a number of levels, providing sound insulation as well as an aesthetic that is more human friendly than concrete alone. The combination of delicate fabrics with brutalist concrete creates an unconventional juxtaposition. At a tactile level, it invites the viewer to touch and experience the differences, hard, soft, cold, warm. It also operates at an environmental level, reducing the need for additional painting or cladding over the concrete. They are researching and testing the acoustic properties of a number of fabrics including cashmere, flocked fabric and lace from Northern Ireland. Specially prepared moulds are used to create panels: the fabric is placed in the mould with cement poured over and left to dry over a period of 28 days.

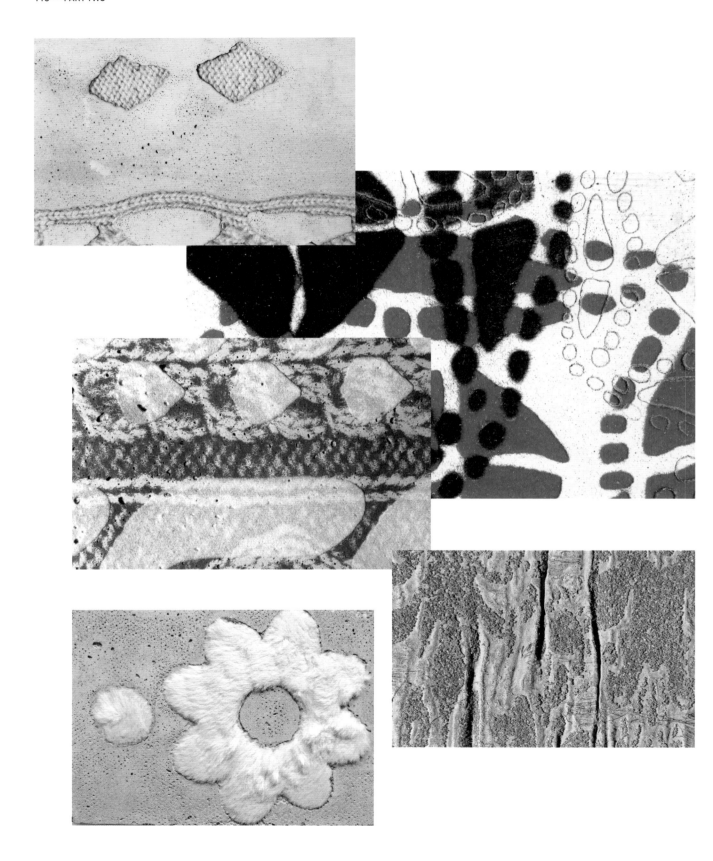

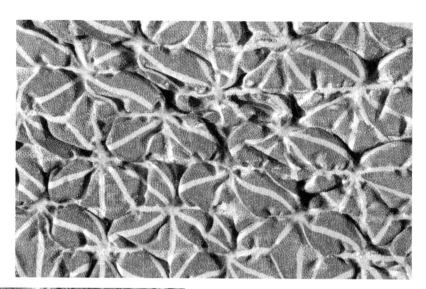

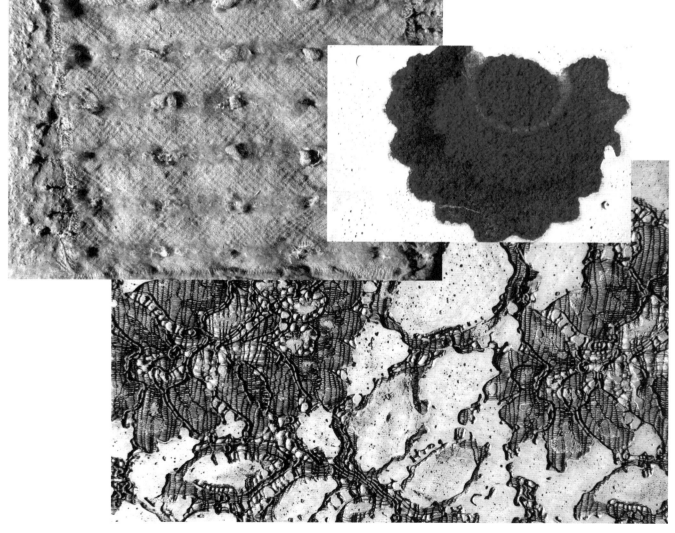

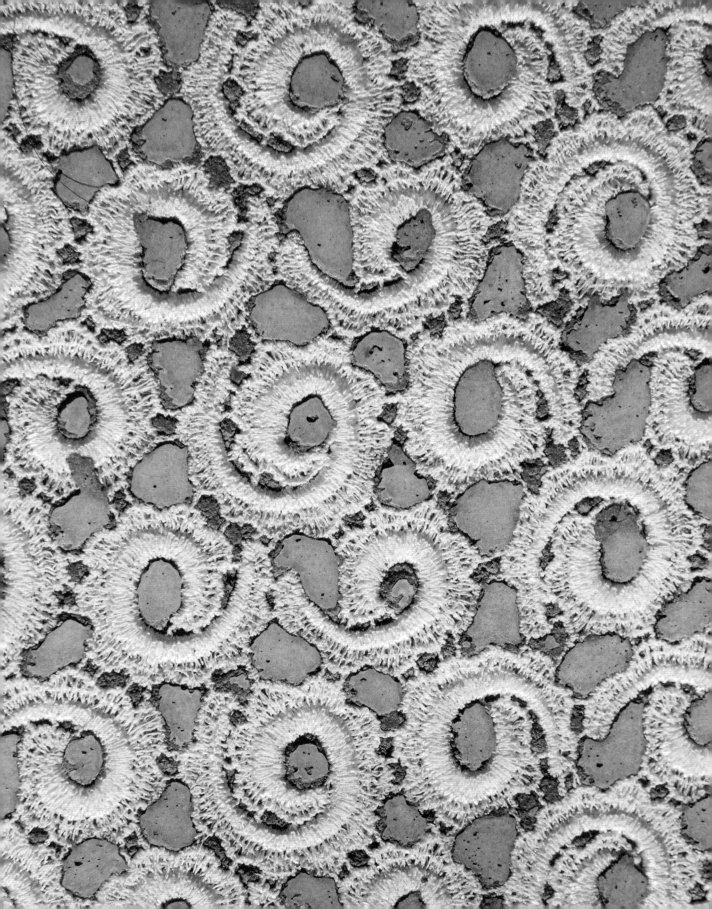

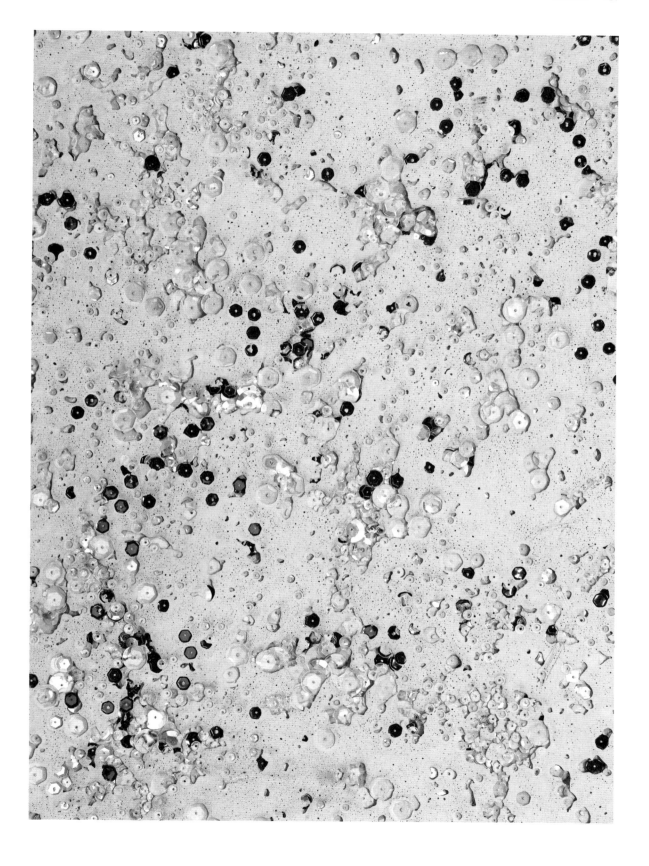

Chamber Music Hall, *Zaha Hadid Architects, Manchester, UK, 2009.* Here the acoustic fabric has also become the stage design as the drape echoes the flow of a dancer's ribbon or the movement of a piece of music.

Zaha Hadid Architects, one of the most consistently innovative architects working today, is exploring this area. In her commission for the Chamber Music Hall for the 2009 Manchester International Festival, Hadid has used fabric as though it is a giant acoustic ribbon curving around and through both the orchestra and the audience. The installation was specifically designed for the performance of J. S. Bach solo partitas and sonatas, to reflect the original intimate setting for which the music was composed. In this contemporary space, Gobelin tapestries have been replaced by a stretch membrane with additional acoustic insulation provided by a series of transparent acrylic panels that act to reflect and disperse sound. The technical problems faced by acoustic engineers Sandy Brown Associates ranged from ambient noise from street traffic outside to the air conditioning systems within the building itself. The engineers looked to achieve a balance between providing enough sound insulation and preventing the acoustics from becoming dry with no reverberation.

The Swiss architects Herzog & de Meuren Architekten AG worked with the Chinese artist Ai Weiwei on the design of one of the most spectacular buildings to appear at the Beijing Olympic Games in 2008. The Chinese National Stadium, more commonly referred to as the Bird's Nest, representing 'heaven', looked to traditional basketry and cracked glazed pottery for inspiration. One of the building's architects Jacques Herzog uses the term 'architectural forest'. The interlaced structure protects a saddle-shaped inner roof clad in a series of ETFE panels on the upper area, with an acoustic PTFE membrane under the steel structure to reflect and absorb noise. The German company Vector Foiltec produced

Chinese National Stadium, Herzog & de Meuren Architekten AG, Engineers: Arup, Beijing, 2008. The building is most commonly referred to as the Bird's Nest. The close proximity of many of the buildings at the Beijing Olympic Games meant that acoustic control was needed to prevent street noise from coming in as well as stadium noise going out and disrupting events outside.

Norwegian National Opera and Ballet House, *Snohetta, Oslo, 2008.* Stage safety curtains provide acoustic insulation and fire protection in theatres. Pae White's jacquard weave with digital image brings a dramatic aesthetic as well as maintaining the necessary protective qualities.

the ETFE for the stadium under the brand name Texlon Foil System. Architectural engineers Arup then worked with the architects to realize the structure, which spanned 313 by 266 m (1026 x 872 ft), seated 91,000 spectators and had to withstand extreme weather, pollution and the threat of earthquakes in one of the world's most active seismic zones. The building is transformed by light with the textile membrane acting as a filter to soften the light coming through during the day and offer a diffuse glow to artificial lighting at night.

HEALTH + SAFETY

Space habitation provides some of the most demanding health and safety requirements. Many of the technically advanced materials that have become commonplace in our lives originated in their research laboratories. Materials such as Mylar, Dacron, Nomex and Vectran can be found providing protection in a wide range of industries from healthcare and transport to architecture.

ILC Dover works with NASA in the research and development of spacesuits, lunar vehicles and habitat. Payload is a primary issue in space travel, and this has motivated research into the use of lightweight, soft, deployable habitats. They must withstand extreme temperatures as well as radiation exposure and space debris. One development is a structure that is mid-expandable: this allows the soft fabric elements to be stored in two hardened domed endcaps during transportation. Deployed on the moon, it would double in size. No single material is being used; instead a sandwich layer combines ten materials, a number of which have been previously tried and tested in space. These include aluminized Mylar, coated Dacron, Vectran webbing and an outer layer of Ortho-Fabric, which combines Gore-Tex, Kevlar and Nomex. Maintaining air pressure in a 3-m (10-ft) diameter inflatable while in space is proving a significant challenge. Antarctic conditions are frequently used as a testing ground for lunar habitats such as this with average temperatures of -30°C (-22°F) and winds that can reach over 100 km per hour (62 miles per hour). Testing goes beyond the actual structure to look at how improvements might be made in packing, transportation and set-up, as well as power consumption in use.

What the space industry refers to as durable advanced flexible reusable surface insulation is in effect thermal insulation blankets. There are two extremes to be faced. The first is the temperature in space that is referred to as absolute zero: -273°C (-459°F) in terrestrial terms. However, the temperature at re-entry (depending on spacecraft speed) is around 1593°C (2899°F). NASA, working with 3M, has developed Nextel, a ceramic thermal insulation blanket. It has the ability to withstand high temperatures and flying debris without deforming on impact as metal fibers do. Weight and bulk are important issues for space travel and the material scores highly on both counts. The material specifications are much higher than required for housing, but it is being used for industrial applications such as lining for porcelain and galvanized steel furnaces.

McMurdo Station, *Antarctica National Science Foundation (NSF)*. Part of a NASA prototype lunar habitat designed by ILC Dover is set up at NSF's McMurdo Station, Antarctica. Conditions of extreme cold, isolation and lack of comfort mirror some of the issues faced by astronauts.

Designing for healthcare and wellness in buildings, Blücher GmbH specialize in the development of filter technologies. Spherical high-performance adsorbers operate in a similar way to activated carbon-eliminating pollutants, smells and other unwanted substances. The adsorbers are integrated between an outer layer of fiberglass and the inner fibrous web. They are highly porous and the structure produces a large internal surface on which filtered substances can be deposited safely. The round particles can be integrated into fabrics for use in applications that include filtration and wall coverings. Saratech Permasorb is a fiberglass wall covering developed as a clean-up system for contaminated buildings. The sorbents for this application have a very high mechanical strength so that even if the covering is damaged, toxins will be prevented from escaping. The wall covering can be installed like wallpaper and once it has decontaminated the masonry it can be removed and disposed of safely.

The German company Future-Shape GmbH has introduced two products to the market that are aimed at helping people and robots through monitoring and sensing. NaviFloor is a radio-frequency identification (RFID) technology that places invisible landmarks on the floor of a building to help robots navigate their way to different locations. The tags work by using an electromagnetic field to retrieve or store information. The robots are fitted with an RFID reader and map to indicate the tag positions. This allows it to determine its exact position as the reader comes in contact with the tag, which is embedded in the underlay of the carpet or parquet flooring. The NaviFloor uses

Cape Town Stadium, *Louis Karol/ Point Architects, Engineers: Schlaich Bergermann & Partners, 2009.* The 68,000-seat stadium has been designed to echo the misty atmosphere of nearby Table Mountain. A translucent Birdair PVC mesh helps to achieve this.

Durban Stadium, *GMP Architects, Engineers: Schlaich Bergermann & Partners, 2009.* Detail of the fold-plate Birdair PTFE-coated glass fiber panels engineered by Schlaich Bergermann & Partners. Two hundred and eight panels were used in the construction. An idea of the scale can be seen by looking at the people on top of the arch who appear ant like.

Cape Town Stadium, *Louis Karol/ Point Architects, Engineers: Schlaich Bergermann & Partners, 2009.* Detail of the sleek tensile roof that results in a shape similar to a large undulating bicycle wheel.

a glass-fiber reinforced fabric and incorporates a standard grid of RFID tags spaced at 50 cm (20 in.) apart. The system allows for detailed data collection such as the date and time of the most recent cleaning operation and even the type of cleaning fluid used. The same company produce SensFloor, designed as a safety monitor for ill and elderly people. The textile-based underlay uses integrated microelectronics and proximity sensors that are activated when people come into physical contact with them. Pattern recognition allows the system to distinguish between footfall and a full body lying on the floor. The alarm is raised in the case of the latter.

SOLAR

Climate control is a major concern in the design of new buildings in addition to systems being retrofitted in older structures. The popularity of large-scale glass-clad buildings, as well as sports stadiums that owners want to use all year round, has created a huge market for climate control in buildings. Unprotected, heat is readily lost in winter, while in summer

Nelson Mandela Bay Stadium, Architectural Design Associates (PTY) Ltd/Dominic Bonnesse Architects, Engineers: Schlaich Bergermann & Partners/Grinaker/ Interbeton JV, Port Elizabeth, 2009. Detail of the 21,000 sq m (230,000 sq ft) Birdair PTFE-coated glass fiber membrane used to form the petals of the undulating roof design for the 50,000-seat venue in South Africa.

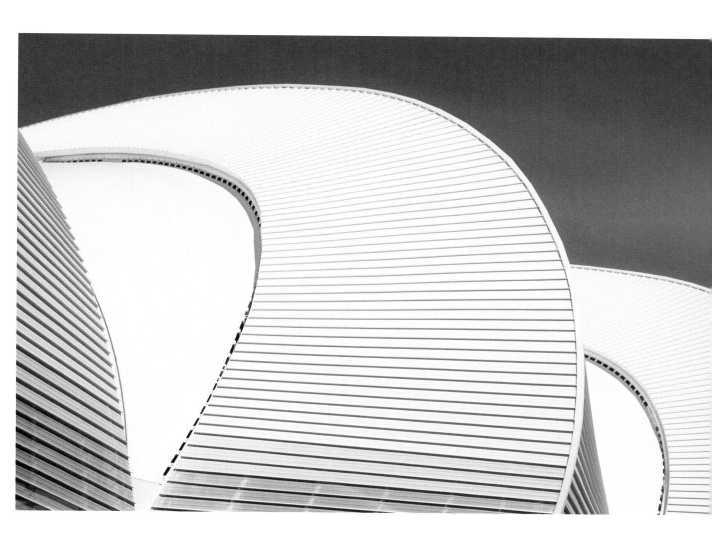

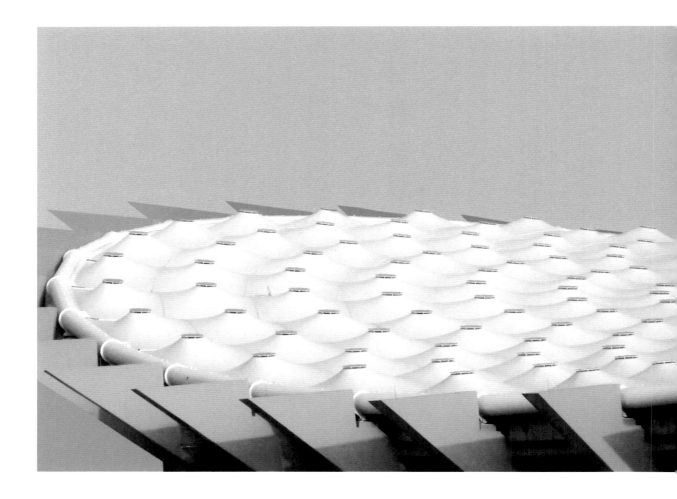

Kuwait National Stadium,
Weidleplan Consulting GmbH,
Engineers: Schlaich Bergermann
& Partners, Safat, 2007. The PTFE-
coated glass fiber membrane is
designed to protect spectators
from the searing desert heat that
can exceed 54°C (130°F).

it is drawn in, making life uncomfortable for occupants. Solar glare is also
a problem as architects look for ways of giving protection without losing
natural light or the view. Architectural membranes offer the ability to
provide shade both for existing buildings and, increasingly, to construct
roof and whole building structures. Large-scale stadiums and Expo
structures have to provide solar shade for visitors without the loss of
daylight. This is posing technical challenges to fabric manufacturers that
include improving sustainability credentials. Expo 2010 Shanghai, as well
as new sports stadiums in South Africa and other countries, has seen some
exciting new architectural and technical solutions emerge.

MakMax is producing two products that utilize sunlight in unique ways.
Their photoluminescence membrane sees a pigment added to the
fabric membrane. While the fabric provides UV protection during the
day, it is also storing sunlight so it can provide a luminescent glow at
night. In a separate development, they are using a titanium dioxide (TiO_2)
coating on membranes that makes the material self-cleaning. This works
by means of a photocatalytic decomposition process which causes an
interaction between the TiO_2 and organic matter, resulting in oxidation

Durban Stadium, GMP Architects, Engineers: Schlaich Bergermann & Ptns, 2009. Offering protection from the sun during the day, the illuminated stadium gives some protection from the cool evening air at night.

Rome Olympic Stadium, Italproggetti S.r.l., Engineers: Studio Technico Majowiwcki, 1990. This is an example of how membranes can be added to existing buildings. The Birdair PTFE-coated glass fiber membrane was added to the original stadium, which was built in 1936.

***Chanel Mobile Contemporary
Art Pavilion***, *Zaha Hadid
Architects, Engineers: Arup,
New York, 2008.* Day and night
views of the touring art pavilion
in Central Park where the sleek
curved form contrasts with its
natural and built surroundings.

so that dirt does not adhere to the surface and is washed away with rainfall. An additional benefit is that it can remove nitrogen oxide (NOx) from the atmosphere: so removing quantities of nitrogen and sulphur from vehicle exhaust emissions, leaving the air cleaner.

When the luxury fashion house Chanel decided to launch a Mobile Contemporary Art Pavilion showcasing the work of 20 international artists, they turned to Zaha Hadid Architects to provide a design that was both contemporary and futuristic. The result is a 700 sq m (7,500 sq ft) complex, organic structure comprised of a series of continuous arched forms with a naturally lit central courtyard. The structure is made from a fiber-reinforced polymer (FRP) which has been toughened with a combination of glass fiber stitched bi-axial fabrics and unidirectional fibers with various core materials. The composite panel structure allows the illuminated building to glow softly at night. During the day, natural light flows into

Burnham Pavilion, Zaha Hadid Architects, Chicago, 2009. The fabric membrane acts as a backdrop to projected images, while providing climate and light control through its louvered roof.

The Norwegian Pavilion, *Helen & Hard, Expo 2010 Shanghai*. The series of 'trees' is made using an environmentally sustainable bamboo and blue glue composite which has been covered with canopies of PTFE-coated ETFE. Sustainable features include a water collection and purification system.

the building through a series of six ETFE sections, roughly triangular in shape. The whole building has been modelled in 3D, including details such as the guttering. Due to the complex curved structure, each of the 400 façade panels is different. The entire pavilion was constructed using minimal materials because it had to be crated and shipped around the world and erected inside a three-week period in each location.

The demands placed on textile structures can sometimes appear conflicting. Hadid's Burnham Pavilion for the city of Chicago had to allow images to be projected on the interior fabric while the outer fabric had to allow the structure to emit a low level of light at night. The design is composed of an intricate curved aluminium structure where each shape has been individually formed and welded to create a deceptively simple yet dramatic form. Textiles have been used as outer and inner skins on the structure with different requirements for each. Fabric Images Inc. provided the textiles using an outer layer of Starfire, a fade-resistant, easy-to-clean material that is most commonly used for awnings and has some water-repellent properties. The inner exhibition area uses a Flag Knit translucent polyester warp knitted for high stretch with a sheer finish which has a good brightness for projections.

Solar shade on the outside or inside of these structures is a popular
solution as it can be fitted retrospectively, often to be extended
when needed and then retracted to let in more light. A flexible solar
shade system was required for the Baltic Mill in Gateshead in the north
of England. The mill dates from the 1950s, but it was it opened as a
major arts venue, the Baltic Centre for Contemporary Art in 2002, having
been significantly remodelled by Ellis Williams Architects and Landrell
fabric engineers who retained as much of the original façade as possible.
To provide solar shade when needed they decided to install a large
sliding door on the exterior made of a PTFE-coated glass fiber fabric.
Hung off the vertical wall of the mill, it has been mounted on a horizontal
track to allow the door to be moved sideways and control the light
entering the gallery spaces. The metal frame of the doors incorporates
stairs for maintenance with 11 pre-stressed panels fitted onto it.

The Expo Boulevard, SBA GmbH,
Engineers: Knippers Helbig Advanced
Engineering, Expo 2010 Shanghai.
PTFE-coated glass fiber membrane
covers an area of 65,000 sq m (700,000
sq ft) and is designed to protect visitors
against changing weather conditions.
The membrane acts as a funnel,
channelling rain and sunlight down
to the base of the structure.

Media-TIC, *Enric Ruiz-Geli with Cloud 9, Barcelona, 2010*. The architects have developed an active tensile façade for climate control with ETFE foils from Vector Foiltec.

Spanish architect Enric Ruiz-Geli with Cloud 9 has designed Media-TIC, located in the 22@Barcelona district of the city. The intention is to provide an environmentally sustainable building that acts as a communications hub and meeting place for the information and communication technology (ICT) industry and businesses. The architect has designed an active tensile façade with the aim of saving up to 20% of carbon emissions. The skeletal structure is clad in an ETFE foil that acts as a dynamic solar filter. The cushions have been designed in a diaphragm configuration kept under constant pressure, but with the possibility of varying air circulation between the layers. The 'air' circulating is, in fact, a combination of air and nitrogen particles creating what Ruiz-Geli refers to as a 'vertical cloud'. Temperature sensors are linked to the system so that it is self regulating. The diaphragm construction makes it possible to control the air circulation between the layers and the degree of shade created. The first layer is transparent, followed by second and third membranes which have a reverse pattern printed onto them. When the two printed layers are inflated and joined together they form a single opaque layer of shade, and when kept apart more daylight is transmitted into the building.

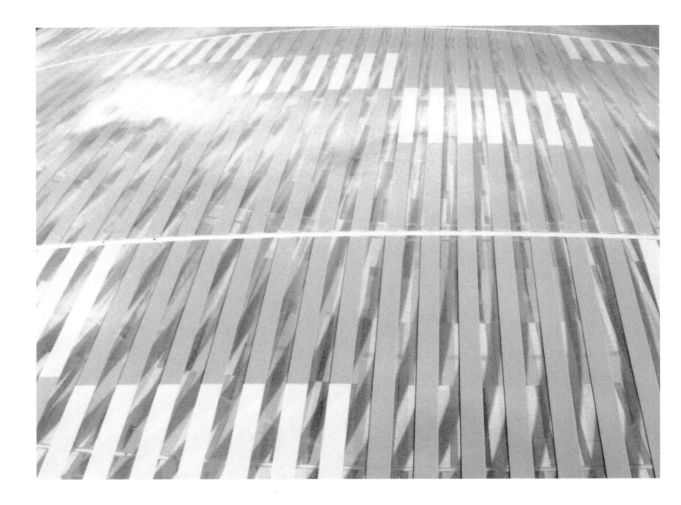

Kingsdale School, *De Rijke Marsh Morgan, London, 2002.* Detail showing Vector Foiltec's variable skin ETFE which allows for greater flexibility in membrane climate control.

The Craig Ellwood-designed Art Center College of Design, Pasadena, has become an architectural icon. In adding a new campus three decades later, the challenge for Daly Genik Architects was how to work with such a strong signature while making their own mark on the architectural landscape. An added challenge was that the building had to be based on a renovation of the old industrial wind tunnel. The solution was to design three sculptural skylights using three layers of ETFE foil, Texlon Vario. Two of the three layers featured printed patterns designed by Canadian graphic designer Bruce Mau. ETFE can be printed or pigmented using fluoropolymer inks: silver is most commonly used because it has the ability to reflect solar light and heat with the degree of solar shade controlled by the density of dots used to create the pattern. The system allows for the two printed layers to move together and apart and in doing this, the light transmittance is altered. This also creates its own aesthetic, softening the hard geometry of the wind tunnel structure. During the day, the pattern creates a dappled effect for students and staff working inside against the strong sunlight. The structure takes on a very different appearance at night as the glow of artificial light is softened when viewed from outside. This is also when the pattern can be most clearly seen.

Although membrane structures can withstand snowloads and other cold climate conditions, they are generally used in moderate to warm climates. With the growing interest and technical advances in green energy, researchers and manufacturers have been looking at ways of integrating some of these energy systems within existing materials and structures. There have been local objections to wind farms because of the newness of the structure. The conventional grey rectangular photovoltaic panels are rarely in keeping with existing roof structures. Manufacturers hope that by bringing together solar technology and membrane structures there will be a greater acceptance of the technology. A number of different processes are being used to apply PV cells to textiles, ranging from flexible photovoltaic-coated fibers to lamination, paint and mechanical processes.

PV membranes are not just becoming easier to install but more autonomous and transportable. This is making them suitable for applications used in disaster relief and leisure industries. PTL Solar is developing a series of products for shade and shelter applications. The PowerPark I is a tensile structure with an integrated photovoltaic system comprised of four power shelters referred to as PowerMods. It uses a single pole support unit for the angled PV, making this a portable and easily erected source of energy. The Canadian company Somfy Systems Inc. has developed Radio Technology Somfy (RTS), which allows the controls and accessories to be operated wirelessly. It includes a wind sensor to detect movement and a solar-powered sun sensor which means the membrane can move automatically in response to environmental changes. Hightex and its sister company SolarNext have developed PV Flexibles, in which thin film solar cells are embedded between two layers of ETFE laminates. The lamination process helps to protect the PV cells from loads and stresses and also allows them to function as shade. ETFE is seen as a more durable alternative to PVC-coated membranes and carries good resistance to UV light and soiling. PV Flexibles and MakMax have both produced membranes that incorporate aerogel for greater thermal insulation.

Vector Foiltec has launched Texlon Solar ETFE cushions which incorporate photovoltaic cells in a laminate on the upper foils of the cushions. The process used to make the cells is continuous roll deposition so that the cells are lightweight and flexible. Each cell is composed of semi-conductor junctions split for maximum efficiency, with the lower cell absorbing red light, the middle one green and top cell blue light. Bypass diodes are connected across the cells so that the modules can produce uninterrupted power even when partially in shade. The product can be incorporated into the Texlon variable skins system to allow for a dynamic climatic envelope. This would mean that solar energy could be harvested, and insulation and light transmittance varied.

The bringing together of function and aesthetic has been very important in the development of textiles for buildings. The process began with the emergence of architectural membranes but is now moving apace to incorporate more dynamic materials and systems that can provide additional protective properties while harnessing energy for a more sustainable future.

South Campus, *Art Center College of Design, Pasadena, Daly Genik Architects, Los Angeles, 2004.* The Vector Foiltec ETFE film has been printed with a design by the Canadian graphic designer Bruce Mau. During the daytime it offers shade from the sun, while at night it is illuminated like a lantern.

TRANSPORT

The way in which textiles are being utilized in transportation has been transformed over the last hundred years or so. Early attempts at flying were doomed to failure as would-be pilots donned what were little more than home-made wings made of fabric strapped to a wooden frame. Few got off the ground, literally. Today, fabric is again being employed, only this time the story is very different. Now textiles are being used in the most advanced aircraft such as Boeing's 787 Dreamliner and the Airbus A350. Both use carbon fiber-based composites to create super-strong lightweight carbon fiber wings with lightweight and ergonomic fabric cabin seating inside the Airbus. The material is not inexpensive so the trade-off is the saving made on weight and consequently fuel running costs.

The use of advanced fabrics in transport can be seen at every level from the weight-saving composites to acoustic and vibration damping and climate control. Designers and engineers are investigating the possibilities these materials can offer in space, in the air, on the seas and on the highways around the world.

WEIGHT

In his book entitled *Lightness*, Adriaan Beukers of Delft University of Technology (TU Delft) emphasizes the importance of the weight to strength ratio in transport: 'now lightness, or performance per energy unit, is quickly gaining in significance again because... cheap energy is getting scarce'. This is taking many forms in the use of textiles for vehicle design, with the primary focus on composites. There are three main approaches in composite design for the transport industry. The first is based on the use of high-strength lightweight fibers such as carbon and glass fibers. The second is looking at the use of natural fibers such as hemp and jute, and the third area starting to emerge is the use of bioresins. The direction of research and development in composites for transport is driven by factors such as cost, sustainability, strength and consumer acceptance. Research and development has also been influenced by initiatives such as the European Union's End of Life Vehicles (ELV) directive which requires that all new vehicles should be 95% recyclable by 2015. The challenge for designers is to find ways of making composites for vehicles stronger and using them to replace heavier and less sustainable metal parts.

Carbon, glass, aramid and polyester fibers are the main textile components of composite materials for transport. Their strength-to-weight ratio is good, making them a viable alternative to heavier metal parts. At the high end of the market the use of advanced composites may have the advantage of adding to the product exclusivity. Carbon fiber composites have been used extensively in the Formula One industry for a number of years and this know-how is starting to trickle through to consumer vehicles. Aston Martin's One-77 is an example of the use of composites at the luxury end of the market. The two-door coupé has a lightweight monocoque body structure made from carbon fiber, which supports a handmade aluminium skin. The luxury car retails at US$ 1.5 million.

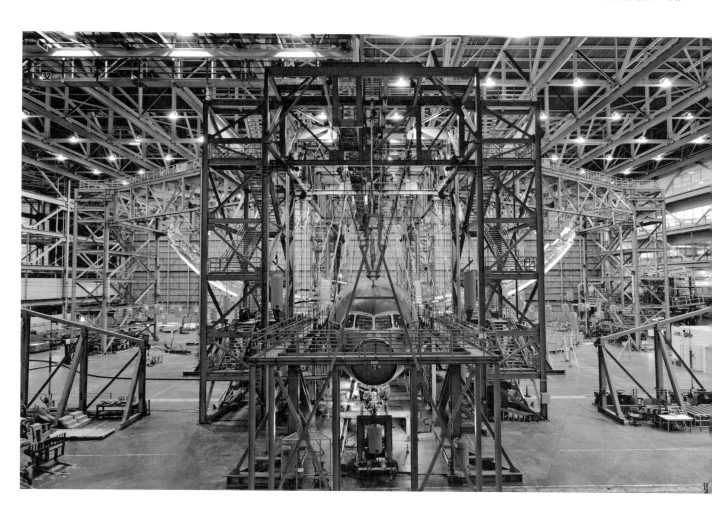

Dreamliner, *Boeing, 2010.*
The ultimate load wing test on
the 787 Dreamliner. The wings were
flexed upwards by around 7.6 m
(25 ft) during the test, with data
collected from sensors each second
over a two-hour period.

WhiteKnight, *Virgin Galactic/Scaled Composites, 2002.* The manned twin-turbojet research aircraft is designed with a lightweight carbon fiber composite for the high altitude airborne launch of SpaceShipOne, a manned sub-orbital spacecraft.

WhiteKnightOne and SpaceShipOne, *Virgin Galactic/Scaled Composites, 2004.* SpaceShipOne or Spaceiphone is a three-plane high altitude research rocket designed for sub-orbital flights up to 60 miles (100 km) in altitude. A pneumatic-actuated feather design allows it to convert into a high drag shape for stable atmospheric entry.

WhiteKnightTwo, *Virgin Galactic/ Scaled Composites, 2008.* Carbon fiber composite construction designed to carry two pilots and six passengers. It is 18 m (60 ft) long with a cabin diameter of 2.25 m (7½ ft). The image shows its third test flight over the Mojave Desert in the USA.

A4 Decoy, *Swissetulle*. A silver-coated weft yarn is looped diagonally around the vertical warp yarn to form a hexagonal mesh in this Bobbinet construction which provides radar reflective properties.

Opposite: ***Advanced airship flying laboratory***, *US Navy, New Orleans, 2010*. The design is derived from the commercial A-170 series blimp, the manned airship is being used here to help detect oil and direct wildlife rescue following the Deepwater Horizon disaster.

Carbon fiber aircraft window,
Institute for Flugzeugbau, University of Stuttgart, 2009.
Prototype of a carbon fiber prepreg to be used as a lightweight aircraft window.

Bayer MaterialScience LLC, suppliers of multi-walled carbon nanotubes, and Nanoledge Inc., developers of epoxy resins, have collaborated with the alternative energy vehicle (AEV) manufacturer Velozzi to develop components for a lightweight hybrid electric vehicle. The resulting Baytubes promise to increase the mechanical strength of the carbon fiber composites by around 40%, reduce the risk of fatigue, and improve impact and compression resistance. Velozzi is using the technology in the development of their new crossover vehicle, the SOLO, which aims to achieve fuel consumption of 100 miles per gallon.

Currently under development is a new type of aircraft, hybrid air vehicles (HAV). Heavily reliant on the use of lightweight membranes for their construction and designed as very heavy lift vehicles, they rely on helium for 50% of their buoyancy. The vehicles incorporate hover cushions instead of wheels so that they can take off and land in inhospitable

terrain. These specialist aircraft are designed for military use, surveillance and humanitarian aid. The British company Hybrid Air Vehicles produces a series of HAVs entitled 'SkyCat'. These are capable of carrying payloads up to 1,000 tons, and operate at a maximum height of 3,000 m (10,000 ft) at speeds up to 120 knots. It can remain airborne for a period of five days. Laminated fabric is used with engineering analysis that looks to architectural membrane diagnostics as much as conventional aviation industry engineers. World SkyCat is another British based company working in this area. Using similar principles, the SkyCat envelope is constructed of heat-bonded, high-tensile fabric laminate which incorporates a Mylar film to provide a protective gas barrier. The payload module uses the DuPont aramid Kevlar as part of a composite material to provide the high strength needed with minimum weight.

Henry Ford once said, 'The most environmentally friendly thing you can do for a car that burns gasoline is to make lighter bodies.' Ford's own experiments with composite alternatives to metal panels for cars included the use of hemp. Though enthusiastic about the results, the early composites did not progress into production. This was largely due to the US introduction of the Marihuana Tax Act of 1937 which effectively destroyed the hemp industry. Today, more sustainable legislation such as the European Union's ELV policy is being introduced. The challenge for the automotive and related technical textile industries is to find ways to make composites for vehicles stronger, lighter and easier to recycle, using them to replace heavier and less sustainable metal parts. The Ford Motor Company's Environmental Sustainability Report 2009–2010 announced, 'We are actively researching and developing renewable material applications that will reduce our overall use of petroleum products and improve our carbon footprint, while providing superior performance.' In 2009 the company estimated that almost 300 parts in their European vehicles were derived from natural materials such as cotton, wood, flax, hemp, jute and natural rubber. They are now working on substituting up to 30% of their glass fiber reinforcement with hemp and sisal for injection-moulded plastics.

Natural fiber-reinforced plastics (NFRP) use fibers such as jute, flax and coir, which are combined with recyclable resins such as polypropylene and polyolefin to produce more sustainable composites. Crops such as hemp and jute are particularly promising in this area because of the fibrous bast or outer sheath of the stem. These strong, long fibers are seen as a viable alternative to E-glass because of the mechanical parallels. There are still many issues to be overcome in this area if these materials are to be used for more structural applications in cars. Fiber degradation, impact strength and fire resistance are some of the issues that researchers are still addressing.

The agricultural machinery manufacturer John Deere & Company has been working with the Affordable Composites from Renewable Resources (ACRES) unit at the University of Delaware, looking at the possibility of using a soybean-based resin in a glass fiber composite. The first product to emerge was a side door using a resin transfer moulding (RTM) process for the John Deere Ottumwa Works round hay baler. The second stage saw a hand lay-up process used to create rear panels for some of the

John Deere Harvester Works' new 50 Series family of combines. Following on from this development, they began to work with the Ashland Specialty Chemical Company to develop a soybean-based polyester resin that could be used in the sheet moulding compound process. The process of research and refinement continues in order to increase the level of soybean and corn as a component of the finished composite. The Harvest Form composite is proving very strong while weighing 25% less than steel: quite a weight saving on a vehicle the size of a combine harvester.

Mercedes-Benz used a jute composite for the inside door panels of their E-Class vehicles and flax/polypropylene components as a substitute for glass fiber in the underbody of the A-Class. Germany's Four Motors GmbH has gone further in their use of natural-fiber composites with their BioConcept Car, which is almost wholly comprised of biocomposites that appear on doors, bonnet, boot lid, mudguards, bumpers and wings. The materials are found to be lighter in weight than glass fiber alternatives and more stable on impact, being less inclined to splinter. The car design is based on the Mustang GT RTD.

BioConcept Car, *Four Motors GmbH, 2009.* The car body is made almost entirely of natural-fiber composites, including the doors, wings, bonnet, bumpers and boot lid. This is the second generation biocomposite car from the group and is based on the Renault Megane Trophy. It is run on biodiesel.

Oman Air Majan, *Boatspeed, 2010.*
The single-skippered 30-m (100-ft)
trimaran maintained an average
speed of 10.081 knots (30 mph)
sailing around the British mainland
and Ireland, some of the most
challenging coastline in the world.

In addition to their environmental benefits, natural fibers can also
offer some performance benefits in certain applications. Researchers
at Loughborough University in England are focusing on the potential
for nonwoven needle-punched hemp matting to reduce the brittleness
of products made using phenolic resin. A double layer of the hemp matting
offers the potential for greater flex strength in the composite as the fibers
help to dissipate impact energy and reduce the number and size of voids
within the structure because of the hydrophilic properties.

SPEED

The weight of materials has a major impact on speed and performance.
Composites are playing a crucial role both for highly competitive races
and for leisure use. Two competitive boats, ABN Amro TWO and ONE,
were built at the same time for the 2006 Volvo Ocean Race. Designed
by Juan Kouyoumdjian and built by Schaap Shipcare, they are largely
similar except for the design of the decking of the ABN Amro ONE, which
skipper Mike Sanderson and his crew strongly influenced. The lightweight
hulls were made using carbon fiber skins and a Nomex honeycomb core.
A special adhesive film is used to bond the honeycomb to the carbon
fiber. Any lack of adhesion results in delamination where the skins come
away from the honeycomb, a problem experienced by other boats in
the race. To reduce the risk of air bubbles, small holes are pricked in the
carbon fiber layers to allow air to escape. To make absolutely sure after
each layer, Schaap packed the hulls in vacuum foil which was then sealed
airtight and the vacuum applied. This removed any air voids that might
still have been present.

In Australia Boatspeed has developed a Custompreg composite
technology which is proving ideal for achieving lighter structures
even at large scale. An in-house computer-controlled impregnation
system allows resin to be applied to the fibers so that the resin content
can be tailored within individual components. The composites can
be strengthened where necessary and less reinforcement applied to

areas where the stress is not likely to be as great. The method helps to maintain a consistent fiber tension even around complex curves while enhancing the core bonding strength and longevity of the laminate. The system has been used for Oman Sail's Arabian 100 Trimaran which measures 32 m (105 ft) in length and a width across three hulls of 16.5 m (54 ft). The giant trimaran promises to be one of the fastest ocean racers ever conceived, capable of speeds in excess of 35 knots (65 kph). Its design focuses on the conditions in the Gulf area and south to Antarctica where wind speeds are often higher than in other regions of the world.

In North America Hodgson Yachts Inc. has designed a very different boat, the 65' Café Racer, also using composites to achieve maximum lightness. The difference in the way the carbon fiber is used is that it appears alongside an Alaskan Yellow Cedar wood. The construction begins with a male mould covered with the wood. Next a sandwich structure of carbon fiber and epoxy resin is applied to the mould using a cold-moulded composite infusion (CMCI) process, and then the core material is heat formed and bonded to the inner skin. The outer laminate is then infused. Much of the Alaskan Yellow Cedar wood is left in place at the end of the process. This is partly for aesthetic purposes, but also to provide some acoustic insulation.

ENERGY

Solar-powered vehicles may still be some way from becoming commonplace, but events such as the World Solar Challenge highlight some of the new innovations in engineered and composite materials, serving as an indication of future trends to watch out for.

In the annual World Solar Challenge race solar-powered vehicles cover the length of Australia, travelling 1,800 miles (3,000km) from Darwin to Adelaide. The event stems from a journey made in 1982 by the Danish adventurer Hans Tholstrup who drove a home-made car fitted with photovoltaic cells across Australia from west to east. The route for the World Solar Challenge takes drivers right through the centre of the country, across some of the toughest terrain and climate conditions in the world. The tightly regulated rules insist that participants can only use solar energy as a source of power. The surface area of the PVs is not allowed to exceed 6 sq m (64 sq ft). The driver has to sit in an upright position and driving is only allowed between 8am and 5pm. The driver must spend the night at the exact location reached at 5pm. These and the many other technical challenges, coupled with the extreme endurance of the race itself, mean that it has become a showcase for the car of the future.

The Dutch Solar Team Twente team have worked with the Dutch textile manufacturer TenCate Advanced Composites on their vehicle. The primary innovation in this design from the team is the use of a tilting wing that can move with the sun, ensuring that the sun's rays are always falling directly onto the solar cells so as to improve efficiency. The composite materials used in the construction are largely derived from the space and aerospace industries. The structural parts of the car use Centex, a thermoplastic glass-reinforced carbon laminate. The curved areas of the car use carbon, glass and aramid textures to reduce the overall weight further without any noticeable loss of strength. The result is a vehicle that is 5% lighter than before: a weight saving of 29%. An additional benefit is that the materials allow for a smoother and more aerodynamic finish, offering 25% less air resistance than earlier designs. The efficiency, weight and positioning of the PVs is crucial to the success of the design. Solar Team Twente use a special Fresnel lens system to capture sunlight from an area of 7.2 sq m (77 sq ft), concentrating it into the maximum surface area of 6 sq m (64 sq ft). The positioning of the PVs also allows for as much sunlight as possible to be captured. The pivoting body that connects the PV panel to the solar car is made from a thermoplastic elastomer that has a similar flexibility to rubber, allowing the panel to tilt so that the wing follows the direction of the sun. TenCate estimate that the combination of the two offers a 25% increase in energy generated.

The Dutch team from TU Delft has won the race four years in succession with their Nuna design. In 2009 their Nuna5 entry measured just under 1 m (3 ft) in height and weighed 160 kg without the driver. Textile composites form the basis for this lightness with much of the car built using carbon fiber and aramid composites, either individually or combined. The car was built at the Schaap Composites shipyard in Lelystad which is also responsible for the ABN Amro ocean race boats. Before being taken to Australia for the race, the vehicle underwent a wind tunnel test at the DNW wind tunnel at Marknesse. In order to gather performance data, liquid paints were applied over the surface of the vehicle to record the flow of air. The results showed a 30% reduction in drag from their previous entry. In terms of fuel consumption, team leader Rein van den Eljnde estimates that if the car were run on petrol 'the whole race of about 3,000 km would require only 23 litres of fuel'.

Sunswift, the solar racing team of the University of New South Wales (UNSW) in Australia, won the Challenge Class Silicon award for vehicles deriving power exclusively from silicon-based photovoltaics. The team use SunPower solar cells which incorporate TopCells to run the telemetry system in their Ivy car, which has been specially developed and built at the university. The cells use the process of encapsulation (developed by Bochum and Solar Technologies) to texture the cells through an etching process. This serves to maximize the absorption of the sun's rays, which are further enhanced by the use of maximum powerpoint trackers and 99% efficient motor controllers. These ensure that as much power as possible is delivered to the wheels, while any surplus energy can be stored in the lithium ion batteries used by peripheral devices.

COMFORT

The average passenger aircraft uses a 50/50 mixture of fresh and recirculated cabin air. In order to save on fuel costs, some pilots have been known to reduce fresh air to as little as 20%. The air is passed through high efficiency particulate arresting (HEPA) filters, which trap most of the microscopic particles as long as they are well maintained. A new AirManager filtration system from Quest International and BAE Systems promises to kill 99% of pathogens.

Boat construction, *Boatspeed,*
Australia, 2010. Using their
CustomPreg composite technology,
Boatspeed is able to build
very lightweight and high-
performing boats for competition
and leisure markets.

PlanetSolar, PlanetSolar, Kiel, 2010.
The images show the multi-hull vessel
under construction at the Knierim Yacht
Club in Kiel. At the time of construction
it was the largest solar boat ever made,
measuring 31 m (102 ft) in length and
15 m (49 ft) in width.

EN-V Concept Car, *General Motors, 2010.* The car is pronounced 'envy' and designed for the driver and a single passenger; in size it is just 1.5 by 1.5 m (around 5 x 5 ft) with a weight expectancy of 400 kg, including the passengers.

The system is based on a Close Coupled Field Technology (CCFT) that uses an electric field to strip electrons from some of the molecules in a gas, allowing biohazardous agents to be captured by an electrostatic filter. The AirManager is intended to kill most bacteria, viruses and other biohazards as well as chemical contaminants, pollutants and bad smells. In a one-hour flight the air is passed through the filter about 30 times.

The increasing use of carbon fiber in aircraft construction brings reduced fuel consumption as its primary benefit. However, the fact that it will not corrode means that the air within the aircraft will not have to be kept so dry. This will reduce the problem of dehydration, particularly on long-haul flights.

Technical textiles are widely used in vehicle interiors, far more than might at first be evident and for a variety of functions. Acoustic and vibration damping are of great concern in all vehicles that have engines. The engines themselves cause noise, as does their proximity to the vehicle parts and body next to them. The outside environment also causes problems, as do the occupants. There is no single solution, but one area of fabric structure is key to solving the problem of insulation – nonwovens. To date, these have been primarily made of polyester because of its ability to be easily formed to shape and, of course, cost. Some new

Sunswift, *University of New South Wales (UNSW), Australia, 2009.* The university's team were winners of the Challenge Class Silicon award for vehicles deriving power exclusively from silicon-based photovoltaics in the 2009 World Solar Challenge race.

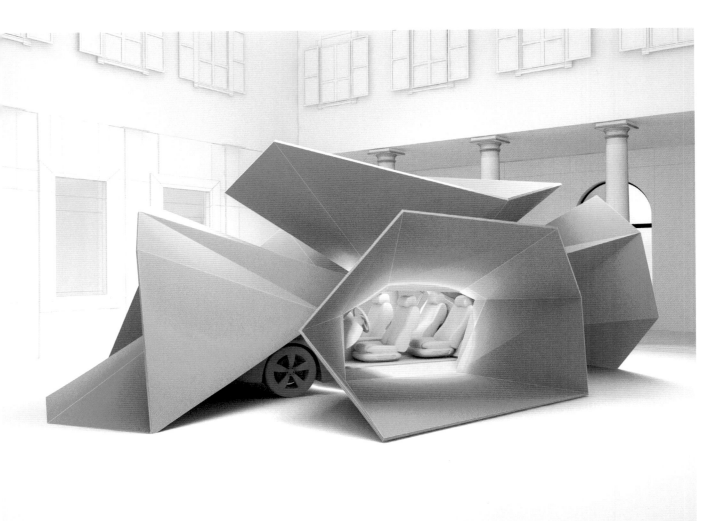

The Dwelling Laboratory,
BMW, 2010. A unique project with
textile manufacturers Kvadrat
and designers Patricia Urquiola
and Giulio Ridolfo. Based on the
5-Series Gran Turismo, the project
explores the changing use of cars
as people spend more time in
them. The installation was shown
at the 2010 Salone Internazionale
del Mobile in Milan.

c-change fabric, *Schoeller AG, Switzerland, 2009.* The Swiss company has developed a c-change membrane based on the fir cone that opens and closes in response to climate change. The technology can be applied to a range of fabrics, including car upholstery.

products are coming to the market: Bekaert is producing metal fibers used to create anti-static carpets for commercial aircraft interiors.

Much of the technology being developed for climate and comfort control focuses on the seat. This makes sense given that this is where those using the vehicle will spend most of their time. Seats that offer adjustable support and heating systems are now becoming common, though research is showing concern over the use of heated seats for men. There is a concentration on the use of electronics to operate these systems at present, although there is also movement towards alternative delivery systems. At one end of the spectrum there is a move to reintroduce more natural fibers such as wool, while at the other there is an even greater integration of technology in the use of silver technology to provide anti-bacterial seating.

Sound quality and distribution within cars is an area that manufacturers are constantly looking to improve on. A new flat flexible laminate (FFL) developed by engineers at Warwick University in the UK is one solution under development. Speakers operate on the principle of converting an electrical signal into sound using a mechanical device. In a conventional system a cone speaker creates a varying magnetic field that in turn vibrates a mechanical cone to produce the sound. The FFL speaker technology promises to do this more efficiently by operating as a perfect piston resonator, producing a wave plane with very high directivity and accurate sound imaging.

427 Helicopter, *Bell Helicopter, USA, 2004.* Seymourpowell redesigned the interior of the helicopter for maximum comfort. The result is a luxury car interior applied to the skies. Ergonomic seating as well as improved acoustics are key features in the redesign.

Spacecraft interior, *Seymourpowell, UK, 2006.* Conceptual interior for Virgin Galactic's VSS Enterprise, based on SpaceShipOne. Ergonomically designed to offer crew and passengers maximum comfort, features include seats that can move to a horizontal position during take off and landing.

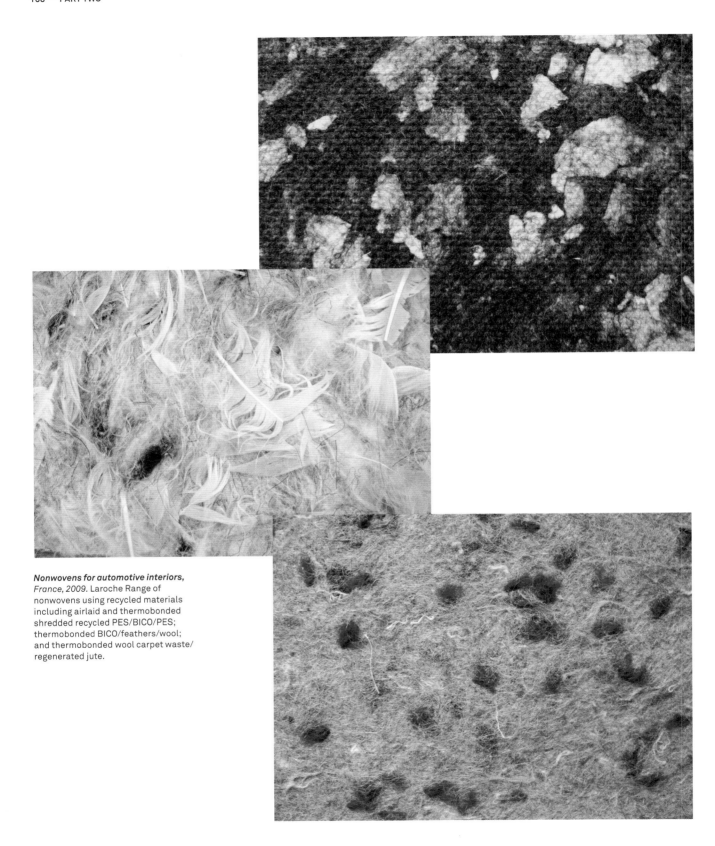

Nonwovens for automotive interiors,
France, 2009. Laroche Range of
nonwovens using recycled materials
including airlaid and thermobonded
shredded recycled PES/BICO/PES;
thermobonded BICO/feathers/wool;
and thermobonded wool carpet waste/
regenerated jute.

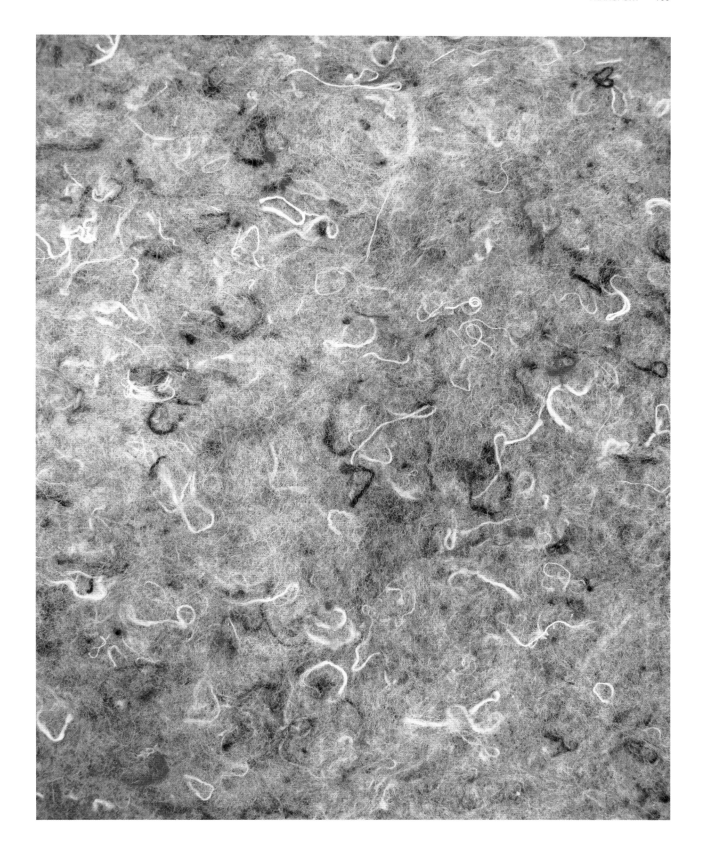

iChange, Rinspeed, Switzerland, 2009.
Concept car with an adaptive energy
concept so that it can respond to
the number of passengers travelling.
The interior comfort is provided by
Schoeller's ColdBlack treatment on
the fabrics to keep the occupants cool.

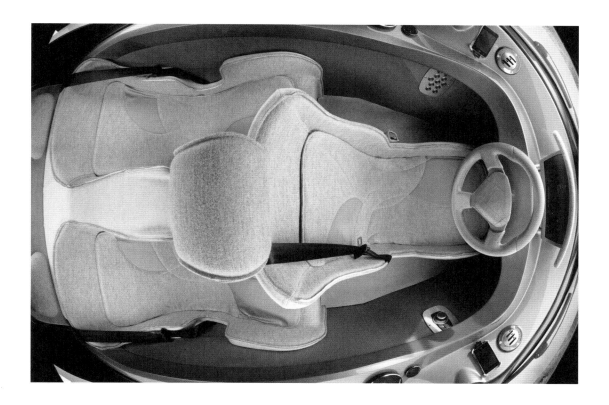

CONCEPT VEHICLES

The concept car acts as a showcase for the latest technologies and futuristic thinking from the automotive industry. They are produced at vast expense for the leading motor shows each year. While there is undoubtedly an air of fantasy about them, most of the materials and technologies used are already on the market. Advanced textiles feature strongly in many of the designs, adding to the aesthetic and performance of the luxury car.

Rinspeed, directed by its owner, the Swiss automotive visionary Frank M. Rinderknecht, consistently produces some of the most stunning concept cars to be showcased each year. The iChange car features an adaptive energy concept so that the body adapts to the number of passengers on board. The car can transform from a streamlined one-seater to a comfortable car for three passengers as the end of the teardrop can expand or contract. The electric motor of the lightweight (1,050 kg) car is powered by lithium ion batteries. The Schoeller Group has produced textiles for the car's interior, providing luxury, comfort and performance. Wool has been treated to give added functionality. The use of the ColdBlack finish on the textiles on the ceiling ensures UV absorption and a pleasant temperature inside the vehicle. Fabric has been braided and gathered, and technical textiles alternate with leather to form three-dimensional shapes. All are designed to look stunning

sQuba, Rinspeed, Switzerland, 2008. Concept car capable of being submerged to a depth of 10 m (33 ft). Interior textiles by Strähle + Hess are designed to dry quickly and to look good in and out of the water.

and to perform. A very different concept car, also from Rinspeed, is the sQuba. The inspiration is pure James Bond: designed to 'fly' under water and is powered by rechargeable lithium ion batteries. The car can be submerged to a depth of 10 m (32 ft) using a range of technologies that include electric motors for underwater motoring and Seabob jet drives (made using carbon nanotubes) which 'breathe' through special rotating louvers. Textiles for the interior have to perform on dry land and underwater – the car is submerged as an open top. Strähle + Hess is responsible for the fabrics that are inspired by the yellowtail snapper. Knitted fabrics are designed with a silver/yellow fish-scale texture. All fabrics have been backed with three-dimensional spacer fabrics, which are open on the inside to help water drain more quickly when the vehicle emerges from the water.

The BMW concept car Gina (Geometry and Functions in 'N' Adaptations) explores the use of fabric to create a shape-shifting car of the future. A Z8 chassis holds an aluminium frame controlled by electric and hydraulic actuators to allow the car to change its shape, over which the fabric is stretched. A polyurethane-coated Lycra-based fabric is used for flexibility, the coating making it water resistant. The fabric is tough but translucent to allow the tail lights to shine through. Motors are fitted so that the fabric over the front headlights can be pulled back to reveal the lights when needed.

Gina, BMW, Germany, 2008. Concept car using polyurethane-coated Lycra-based fabric skin to show how cars of the future could be made not just of textile composites, but also of soft fabric.

Light Car, *Open Source, EDAG GmbH, Germany, 2009.* Concept car with a strong environmental philosophy as the designers use a basalt fiber composite for the body which is fully recyclable and naturally flame retardant. In making it, Open Source has engaged the wider automotive and automotive textile community in developing the concept to production stage.

Metamorphosis provided the inspiration for the Teijin Group's electric concept car, PUPA. The Japanese company designed the vehicle to reflect their vision of car designs in 2020. The car's weight is half that of a conventional electric vehicle, largely due to the extensive use of advanced textiles. Carbon fiber composites form the core structure with a reduction in the number of parts made possible by the use of modularized parts made with single-piece moulding. Inside the car a bio-derived polyester is used for interior trim and seating while the tyres use a tyre cord made from Teonex polyethylene naphthalate (PEN) fiber.

Sydney is used to a great many boats sailing into its harbour, but it had never seen anything quite like the Plastiki, which arrived in July 2010. The brainchild of David de Rothschild, the boat was designed by Andrew Dovell of Dovell Naval Architects. The intention was to design a boat using plastic bottles to sail across the Pacific Ocean from San Francisco. In the final design, 12,500 plastic bottles were used. They are in two primary forms: in the first they are sealed under pressure (provided by dry ice) and used for buoyancy. In the second a new material, self-reinforced PET (srPET) produced by Seretex, is used.

The potential for recycled plastic bottles to become textiles first came to public attention in the early 1990s when the sportswear company Patagonia introduced their PET fleece fabrics. Lightweight and warm, they have proven very popular with consumers over the years. In srPET two fibers are used in the weave. The first is a fiber and the second acts as a resin, with two different melting points, allowing them to bond as a material. Cured under compression at 200°C (392°F), they offer a material that is very similar to a medium grade fiberglass in terms of performance. While Dovell has worked on a number of boats for the Round the World Yacht Race, he has no plans to design one based on this new material just yet. However, he is working on a design for a sea kayak using srPET.

The consumer, it would seem, wants everything. This pushes designers and engineers at every level. After all, what is used by the space industry or luxury concept car today may well appear in our public transport systems tomorrow. It seems that we can all benefit from such developments.

Plastiki, Plastiki, USA, 2010. The project demonstrates the impact of our waste on the environment and shows how, with a little ingenuity, there might be no such thing as waste. The boat uses compressed plastic bottles for flotation and srPET, also made from recycled plastic bottles, in composite for the deck and cabin areas.

'Safety Gear for Small Animals', *Bill Burns, USA.* The collection highlights the impact that we are having on the wellbeing and lives of small animals. Miniature versions of real human safety gear are used, including a bullet-proof vest, a hard hat and a triage tent.

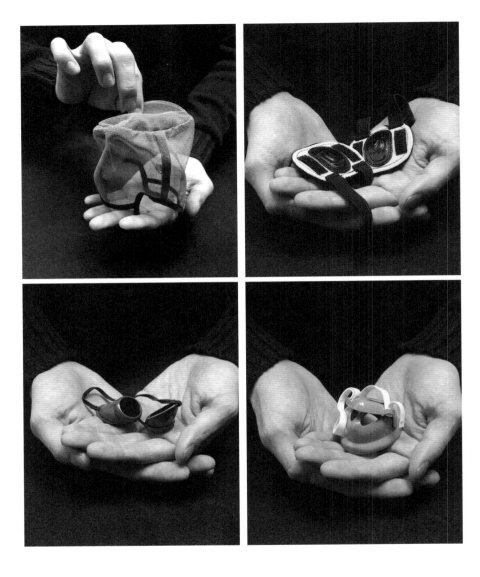

In the Cinderella fairytale we see the heroine's rags transformed into clothes of gold and silver at the touch of a magic wand. One key difference between the children's story and today's researchers and designers is that the latter are delivering a reality not a fantasy. For many adults, whether growing up with magical tales such as these or those of more contemporary action superheroes, there remains a deep-rooted desire to raise our lives to some elevated state through the wearing of fantastical clothes. The Belgian bespoke menswear tailors Scabal is weaving gold into fine cloth and making it into men's suits in a way in which Rumpelstilskin would have delighted. However, it is another Belgian company, Bekaert, who is weaving metals into cloth that will protect the wearer from danger. Both have a restorative function to perform and, increasingly, we are seeing this matched by the aesthetic qualities of the finished garment.

Designers and manufacturers are proving only too happy to oblige in helping make our fantasies a reality. The astronaut is seeing the spacesuit

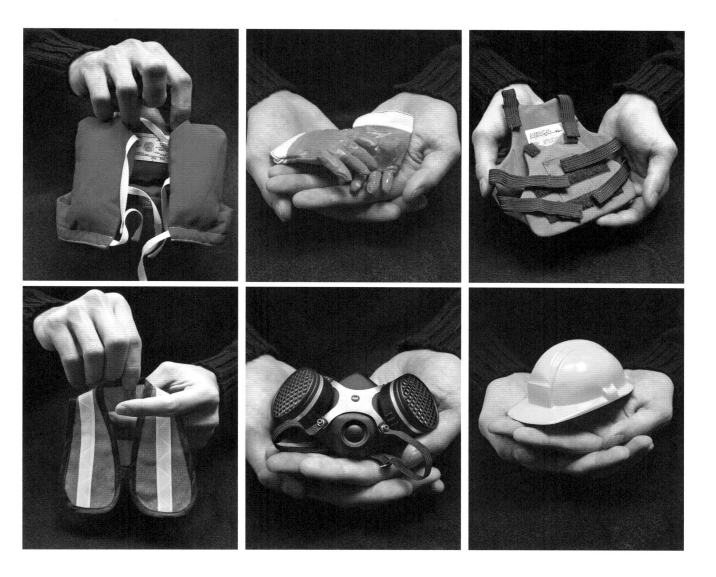

become more comfortable and easier to move about in, even looking
to help the body maintain muscle tone while in space. Terrestrial work
environments can be extremely demanding and often not without
risk. Performance here is being married with the need for improved
visual and tactile aesthetics, important if the worker is to wear the
clothes as intended. In medicine there is a growing trend towards
more out-patient care, especially among elderly people. Here, there is
evidence of clothing being used as a lifeline, literally, as it senses and
communicates patient health and welfare to the primary healthcarer.
Sports is focusing on climate control and garment construction, which it
has allied to futuristic aesthetics in the fabrics and overall design. These
clothes scream success as one brand boasts to have developed clothing
that is more ergonomic than skin itself. The fashion and leisure sectors
can be seen to be the drivers behind a strong push to bring together the
traditional and technological, particularly in the hybridization of natural
and synthetic to the benefit of both.

Underwater spacewalk, NASA, USA, 2009. In the waters of the Neutral Buoyancy Laboratory near NASA's Johnson Space Center, STS-129 mission specialist Robert L. Satcher, Jr is dressed in a training version of his extravehicular mobility unit (EMU) spacesuit as he trains for a spacewalk in preparation for working outside the shuttle.

A soldier goes into combat enveloped in a camouflage battlesuit that renders him completely invisible to his enemy. Elsewhere another soldier is injured, but his clothing allows him to render part of it rigid, acting as a splint, while a remote diagnosis allows the release of the appropriate medicines from his clothing into his bloodstream... This could be a scene from the latest science fiction film, but it is not. These are technologies in varying stages of development from different sources for future military clothing. When we consider that science fiction writers use current research and innovation in industry as their primary source of inspiration, it is hardly surprising that much of what is actually happening outstrips the imaginings of fiction. Consider that by the time the fantasy reaches the big screen the chances are it will already have been realized in some shape or form somewhere in the world.

SPACE

Fritz Lang's silent classic *Woman in the Moon* (1929) contains some quite accurate predictions about space travel, such as the thrust necessary to propel a rocket into space and zero gravity. Less realistic were the crew's clothes, which looked more suitable for a bracing hill walk than a journey to the moon. Much of the depiction of space travel in the film was the result of Lang's discussions with Germany's leading rocket (though not clothing) expert Hermann Oberth. The space industry has been at the forefront of much of the new material and garment construction developments. Many developments that have started with applications in space have also found a ready need on Earth.

The early Apollo astronauts had three custom-made spacesuits each to support their mission. NASA is behind the research and development of the spacesuit, but does not actually make them. ILC Dover is the company behind many of the developments and implementation of the technologies for the spacesuit. As the company succinctly puts it on their web site, 'We created the spacesuit', and it was one of their suits that was worn by Neil Armstrong on the historic first moonwalk in 1969. One of the most important garments to be designed, the extravehicular mobility unit (EMU) has undergone further refinement over the years.

Grado cooling system, *Grado Zero Espace, Italy.* Adapting space technologies and materials for terrestrial applications, Grado Zero Espace has developed this cooling garment for the McLaren Formula One team.

Silver Bio-Suit mock-up,
a collaboration between
Professor Dava Newman,
MIT, Guillermo Trotti, A.I.A.,
Trotti and Associates Inc. and
Dainese. In this collaborative
design project, computer
modelling based on the body's
lines of non-extension has been
used to create an exoskeleton
that supports the body without
unduly restricting movement.

As its name suggests, this is worn by the astronaut while moving about outside in space. The Shuttle EMU consists of 19 pieces and takes 15 minutes to put on, needing the help of fellow crewmembers in the final stages of assembly. The items include a liquid cooling and ventilation garment (LCVG) with tubes of cooling water being continuously pumped around the body. From the inner to the outer layer, the Mercury astronaut wore: an inner liner next to the skin; LCVG; pressure garment bladder made of a urethane-coated nylon; pressure garment cover restraint made of Dacron; TMG liner made of a neoprene-coated nylon ripstop; TMG insulation layers made of an aluminized Mylar, and finally the TMG cover made of an ortho fabric. ILC Dover has also been developing a number of shape-morphing technologies that can be used in spacesuits. These include components such as pneumatic tendons, nasic cells and manual cord adjustment. The intention is that these will allow the spacesuits to be altered easily during flights so that one size can literally fit all.

Technology transfer has been an integral part of the space industry remit both at NASA and the European Space Agency (ESA). The Italian company Grado Zero Espace has been working with the ESA to prototype and help realize commercial applications for some of their leading technologies: one of which is aerogel, the lightest solid in the world. In its purest form the silica aerogel can float on air. Its main benefit is its high thermal insulation so that it can keep the wearer much warmer with less bulk than conventional padding. The material is notoriously difficult to handle so that it is sometimes referred to as 'liquid smoke'. The challenge for Grado Zero Espace has been how to incorporate the aerogel into a fabric so that it can be used in apparel. The result is the Aerogel Design System, where the insulating material has been introduced to a padded fabric that can be used as a liner in jackets and other clothing.

NASA, MIT and Dainese have come together to develop a new concept for space travel. The Bio-Suit System looks to provide astronauts with a second skin in a skin-tight garment that uses elastic tension rather than gas to achieve pressurization. The intention is to offer a life-support system that is a simplified version of existing designs and can help conserve the astronaut's energy as well as reducing the risk of depressurization and other extravehicular activity (EVA) hazards. At the centre of the design is a set of pattern lines that correspond to the body's lines of non-extension – that is the lines of the skin that don't extend when the body moves. The design uses an array of wrapping techniques based on computer modelling of people and, in particular, how their skin behaves during motion. The corresponding lines on the Bio-Suit form what is in effect a stiff exoskeleton to support the body, while also allowing the body maximum flexibility. In order for the suit to be worn by astronauts in space, it must provide almost one third of the pressure exerted by the Earth's atmosphere, around 30 kilopascals (kPa). The prototypes are close to achieving this. Astronauts currently lose around 40% of their muscle strength during space flights. Two additional benefits of the new designs are that by offering varying degrees of resistance, the Bio-Suits offer the possibility of helping the astronauts exercise in space as well as having terrestrial applications in physiotherapy and sports training.

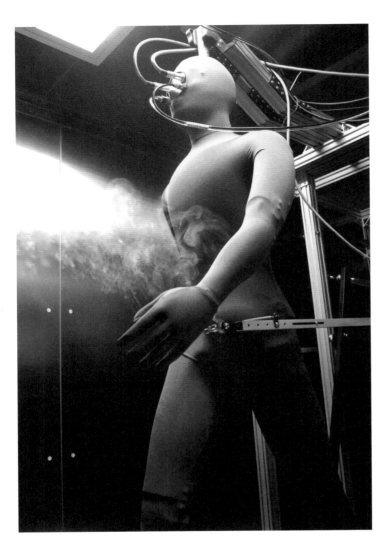

Thermal mannequin, Centexbel, Belgium. The research institute undertakes various tests for clothing including this mannequin which makes a thermophysiological comfort assessment on garments.

WORK

Early film footage of the construction of the Empire State Building in New York during the 1930s shows workers in cloth caps and civilian clothing moving with skill and agility high on the 102-storey building. Built under these conditions and with a workforce of over 3,000, it is astonishing that the death toll during construction was only an unfortunate five. Today's construction workers and those in other high-risk professions are far better protected, physically and legally. There are a number of contributing factors, including a greater awareness of immediate and long-term hazards, as well as the growth of a sophisticated protective fabric and clothing industry.

Protective workwear is tightly regulated with strict industry standards. The fabrics and then the finished garment have to undergo scrutiny. Industrial mannequins have been developed to enable much of the testing to be done on human-like models. The development of testing mannequins has come from the need to evaluate garment performance as well as comfort, particularly with regard to obtaining a thermophysiological measurement. Centexbel has developed a thermal and sweating mannequin which is installed at their research centre in Belgium. It is made using a thermally conductive carbon fiber composite to fit a standard medium size garment. Twenty-six independent zones are monitored using a system of sensors and heating wires. Accuracy is achieved to plus or minus 0.1°C even on wet-skin simulation. In order to provide conditions that are as realistic as possible the mannequin includes movement simulation. It is possible to test most performance fabrics on the mannequin with the exception of certain smart or responsive materials that change when subjected to heat, such as phase change materials (PCMs) and shape memory materials.

DuPont has developed a testing mannequin called Thermo-Man. It was designed to undertake heat and flame retardancy testing to evaluate heat and burn injuries. While the flame retardancy of fabrics such as DuPont's Nomex has been proven, the garments designed using the fabric must be individually tested to check that standards are maintained in the design and construction of areas such as the seams and openings. The imposing Thermo-Man is just over 2 m (6 ft) in height. It is a fully instrumented, high temperature system with 122 heat sensors used to test garments using flash fire conditions. The process is truly impressive as the fully dressed mannequin is literally engulfed in flames.

Protection against their environment is a constant rather than occasional requirement for some workers. For instance, employees working on high voltage lines need complete protection from electricity. Bekaert's Bekinox stainless steel fibers are being used in garments where they can provide protection against electrical and electromagnetic fields. The metal fibers can be produced as a hybrid yarn, with either polyester or cotton making them pleasant to wear and easier to wash. Just as the demands on the performance of workwear are increasing, so too are corporate requirements. The energy company E.ON Energie, with fabrics from W. L. Gore & Associates Inc., has introduced a two-tier clothing system that looks exactly the same but performs differently. Two sets of requirements have been met, but the all-important corporate branding and outward appearance remain the same. Image and Plus are the two clothing lines. Each consists of a series of individual garments: a work jacket, an overall, trousers, bib-trousers, a work coat, a waterproof Gore-Tex jacket and a breathable Windstopper Soft Shell thermal jacket. The Image range is intended for employees in facility management or hydropower plants who need some weather protection but not heat or flame retardancy. The Plus line provides additional protection and is specifically designed for workers in more exposed environments where there is a risk of flame or electric arc exposure.

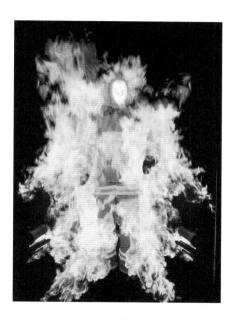

Thermo-man mannequin, *DuPont, USA.* The mannequin is designed to test not just the fabric, but the whole garment construction for flame retardancy.

It is widely acknowledged that people work better if they are comfortable in their clothing. This is especially important for workers in areas that are physically demanding, such as hazardous environments, and those in the emergency services. Lives, sometimes even their own, may depend on their performing to the best of their ability. Clothing that provides protection and comfort is vital. ILC Dover has developed a range of protective clothing, including the Chemturion suit for use in toxic chemical environments. It is intended for workers in extreme conditions where one exposed breath could literally kill them. The Chemturion is made from Cloropel (chlorinated polyethylene) with a clear vinyl visor that allows the wearer 300° vision. Air is fed into the suit via an umbilical-cord-like feeder. To maintain worker comfort levels, a positive air pressure is maintained through four exhaust valves located in the legs and upper back region. The air distribution in the suit is metered to cool the arms and legs, while a spray bar in the hood allows washing, breathing, cooling and defogging with a noise suppressor that enables normal communication through the wall of the suit.

Firefighters and emergency services workers can be at risk from extended exposure or physical activity. The nature of their work and the fact that the lives of others may depend on them, means they may continue to work unaware that their own lives are being endangered. PROeTEX is a European research and development project extending from the WEALTHY (the Wearable Health Care System project), which is an EU project headed by Smartex in Italy with the consortium coordinated by the University of Cagliari. Its aim is to develop smart clothing for workers in extreme conditions to monitor their health via integrated sensors and a communications link to ensure that they are working within reasonable limits. A series of three prototypes is being developed with each incorporating a greater functionality than the previous iteration. Heart and breathing rates are monitored along with body temperature. Progressive prototypes include levels of oxygen in the blood and biochemical measurements of sweat to check for dehydration.

MEDICAL

Richard C. O'Sullivan, chief economist of the Forbes Group, made the observation in 2004 that assisted living was the fastest-growing housing sector in the USA, growing at a rate of 15–20% per annum. This has had the knock-on effect of lowering the rate of in-patient care while increasing the need for out-patient and home care. Designers and manufacturers have been quick to recognize and act on emerging market needs. The result is the development of a series of new and innovative medical products based on a combination of technical textiles and smart materials and systems.

One of the developing product areas relating to out-patient care is effective remote monitoring. The American company VivoMetrics produce LifeShirt, a smart remote wearable monitoring system. It is designed to allow patients to go about their daily routine while being monitored remotely for more than 30 vital life-sign functions. The data is transmitted

Tychem, *DuPont, USA.* The Tychem suits offer chemical and vapour protection for workers in a range of hazardous work environments using a system of multi-layered laminated fabrics.

SeaAir Survival Suit, *Helly Hansen Pro, Norway.* Designed with SINTEF Helse for offshore workers during helicopter transport and as a survival suit in the event of a sea crash or oil platform evacuation.

Trans-For-M-otion, *Eunjeong Jeon,
Curtin University, Australia.* A kinetic
garment using engineered felted
wool and LEDs to give the wearer
a sense of emotional and physical
wellbeing through the change of
the structure in terms of its visual
appearance and shape. Jeon's PhD
research is linked to an Australian
Research Council (ARC) linkage
project 'Innovative Solutions for
Wool Garment Comfort through
Design' supported by DAFWA
(Department of Agriculture and
Food, Western Australia).

to the healthcare professional monitoring the patient's wellbeing.
Garment sensors include respiratory bands and electrocardiography
(ECG) to record electrical activity in the heart with the further
possibility of integrating sensors to monitor skin temperature,
blood oxygen saturation, blood pressure and galvanic skin response.

Centexbel in Belgium is leading an EU-supported monitoring system
aimed specifically at sedated or anesthetized patients undergoing
a magnetic resonance imaging (MRI) examination. It has been
suggested that the MRI scan can yield distorted results because
of the presence of conductive metallic wires in the equipment. There
have also been reports of patients' skin being burnt in the process.
The Centexbel consortium is looking to develop OFSETH (Optical
Fibre Sensors Embedded into Technical Textiles for Healthcare).
This would enable pure optical, rather than electric, sensors to be
used for medical textiles, arguably yielding more accurate results and
reducing the incidence of burns to the skin.

Biochemical sensors form the basis of health-monitoring clothing
being developed by Biotex. Led by the Centre Suisse d'Electronique et
de Microtechnique SA (CSEM), this is another European consortium.

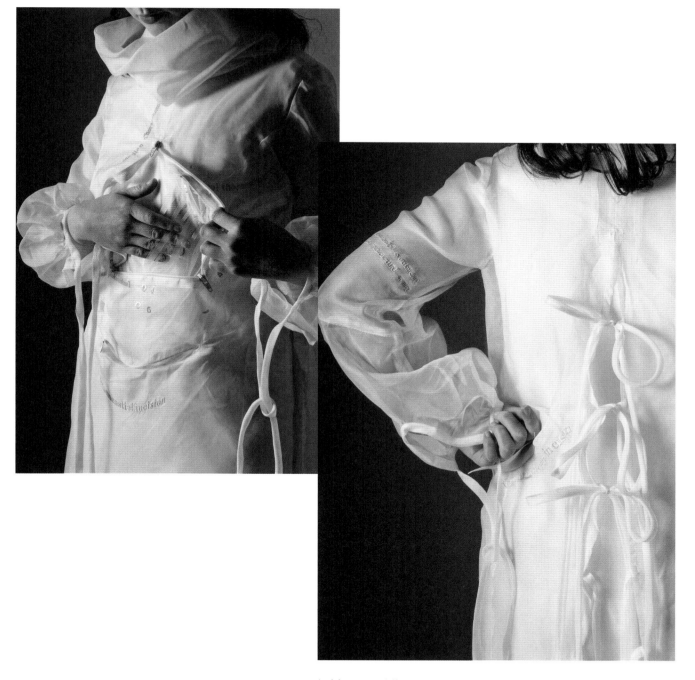

Incision garment, *Karen Fleming, University of Ulster, UK.* The nonwoven garment is a training tool for surgeons, giving them a greater empathy towards their patients than is allowed with a virtual system.

Pre-cool vest, *Nike, USA*. Designed for competitive sports training in hot weather, particularly pre-competition when athletes are trying to acclimatize to hot or humid weather conditions. It was originally developed for use during the 2008 Olympic Games in Beijing.

The technology here is intended to be incorporated into a 'sensing patch' on a textile substrate. This could provide a range of information including oxygen levels in the blood and the detection of infection through bodily fluids. Studies into suitable yarns are leading the consortium to consider hollow fibers as well as hydrophobic and hydrophilic yarns that could help to collect the fluids. The consortium sees possible applications in the monitoring of transplanted organ rejection, wound healing, diabetics and the health status of obese children. Although these technologies are still at the development stage, scientists are already looking further into the future where nanofiber-based sensors could find new applications in the bloodstream, delivering highly detailed information and mapping precise locations on and within the body.

In 1632 Rembrandt painted *The Anatomy Lesson of Dr Nicolaes Tulp.* The striking painting shows teacher and students standing over a cadaver, the subject of their lesson. Today's training for surgeons is not so illicit, though there is a need to give students more experience of what it is like to operate on a real rather than a virtual person. The University of Ulster's Professor Karen Fleming has developed a garment that is designed to act as such a training tool. She has designed a garment with various openings and fabric simulations of primary incision areas to be worn by medical students in their training. The idea is that the students can 'operate' on their colleagues, giving them a greater emotional sense of engagement, as the garment is worn by a living and breathing human being and by someone they know.

SPORT

'A single leg of the [Volvo Ocean Race] course lasting 30 days is the equivalent of 10 years of use for clothing worn by the average person,' according to Karl-Einar Jensen, Marketing Manager of Watersports for Helly Hansen. Many of the world's leading sportswear manufacturers trial their new developments at competitive events such as this, pitching themselves against their strongest competitors.

Successful products help to bring home the trophies and medals for the competitors, while launching products into high street shops for the manufacturing brands. It is sport's equivalent to the fashion industry's catwalks.

Performance, comfort and styling are inextricably linked. Testing facilities for air and water drag are used, but much of the development comes down to what works. It is no coincidence that this is an industry where many of the leading brands were started and are still largely operated by sports practitioners themselves. Surfing and wetsuit design is one of the best examples of this.

Jack O'Neill started his company, O'Neill, on America's West Coast in 1952. A keen surfer, he decided to go into the wetsuit business when he sold some neoprene vests he had been glueing together in his garage to other surfers. The search for the ultimate warm yet lightweight and flexible wetsuit has led to a number of innovative designs. O'Neill has utilized an UltraFlex XDS neoprene with X-Foam, which is insulating yet lightweight and flexible. It is used in the Psycho 2 Hooded wetsuit where it is combined with a number of other high-performance features that offer the surfer greater comfort. A Firewall Insulation jersey fabric wicks moisture away from the body, helping to increase warmth. The knee area utilizes a compression resistant neoprene which is coated with a silicone rubber to give it a more ergonomic fit. A pullover internal neck seal helps to block out water, while a code-red zip with a urethane-coated webbing acts as a further seal and is protected by a double super-seal around the neck. Significantly, the large neoprene panel at the rear of the wetsuit has been made seamless. This is because surfers spend quite a bit of time sitting on their boards and this will reduce the amount of water that gets through. These details develop because the designers use the products themselves and so know what makes a good wetsuit.

The Australian surf label Rip Curl was started by two surfers, Brian 'Sing Ding' Singer and Doug 'Claw' Warbick in 1969. They started the business from the area where they lived and surfed. Their idea was simply to provide wetsuits that were better suited to local conditions around Bells Beach in Victoria, where the surf is some of the most challenging in the world and weather some of the coldest anywhere in the world. The company mantra is 'lighter, warmer and more flexible' with each new design looking to offer significant advances on the last. The H-Bomb series is the world's first power-heated wetsuit. A carbon fiber conductive element is placed in the wetsuit and powered by two low batteries weighing 240 grams to give between one and a half and two and a half hours' heating depending on the setting. Deciding where to place the heating element was a crucial factor. It had to be in an area that would allow maximum fast delivery to the rest of the body and also not interfere with the surfer's movement. They decided that the centre of the back was the most appropriate area, using a titanium backing on the E3 neoprene to reflect the heat onto the body.

A quite different, but equally rigorous set of requirements is needed by yachtspeople, particularly those competing in the world's more challenging races where conditions can change quickly and dramatically.

Rip Curl testing their H-Bomb-heated wetsuit in the chilly waters around the Arctic Circle. A lithium battery powers the heating element in the back area which allows for maximum circulation with minimum bulk interfering with movement.

Girls classic shorti wetsuit, *Rip Curl,*
Australia. Durable, lightweight and
flexible neoprene is only part of the issue
in wetsuit design. Comfort is also a major
factor. With this in mind, the flatlock
seams on this wetsuit allow for the fabric
to be sewn with minimum bulk, while the
pattern has been cut to allow the arms
and shoulders to be seamless.

The Volvo Ocean Race is one of the most demanding
endurance competitions in the sailing world.
Sailing through so many different climates, the
demands on the crew and their clothing are rigorous.
Helly Hansen supply clothing to the Ericsson
racing team. The focus of warm weather clothing
is UV protection, but it is the cold weather clothing
that proves particularly challenging for the design
team. The protection begins with a base layer
of LIFA stay dry technology, a polypropylene wicking
fabric. The mid-layers are windproof and must
also act as a barrier to stop moisture seeping
back towards the base layer. Having trialled lighter
fabrics for the outer layer, it was decided that
the crew preferred some bulk to provide greater
comfort, so a waterproof but breathable Helly Tech
XP fabric is used. Also concerned with the rigours
of the high seas, the British company Musto
is one of the leaders in this area. Their HPX fabric
and garments incorporate a stretch Gore-Tex
Ocean Technology membrane for the ultimate
in waterproof, wind-resistant and breathable fabric
technology. The MPX variation offers many of the
same properties, but in a lighter weight of textile
for less extreme conditions. However, the fabric
is only part of the story. Musto's Gore-Tex Ocean
Drysuit is designed to give up to three hours' survival
time in water temperatures of 5°C (41°F). It comes
with an oral inflator for insulation, protective latex
neck and wrist seals, abrasion-resistant Cordura
seat and knee patches, pocket hand warmer and
a water-deflecting inner lip on the thigh pockets.

Climate control is also key to a number of
developments used in training or pre-competition.
Nike has developed a PreCool vest that was
successfully used in the soaring temperatures
of the 2008 Olympic Games in Beijing. The vest
comprises two layers: the inner layer is like
a giant flexible ice block in triangular formation
and is filled with ice. The fabric on the outer layer
is coated with aluminium, acting like a thermos,
trapping in the cold and reflecting radiant heat.
The idea is to have the competitor's body
temperature cool prior to an event located in a
hot climate. Members of Australia's 2008 Olympic
team took advantage of a cooling vest from Arctic
Heat Australia. The vest incorporates a viscose
gel and can either be put in water at the temperature
required or placed in a freezer and towel dried
before use. Tests show that the Arctic Heat vest
retains its temperature for two to three hours.
Like the Nike vest, it is also used pre-competition.

In sports and fitness training there is a concern to develop muscles, both for strength and to allow sports people to train for longer. Compression suits have been developed to improve endurance, increase strength and power, reduce post-exercise muscle soreness and improve body temperature control. The Australian company Skins has developed a range of compression suits that do just that and they are being used in a wide range of competitive and endurance sports. Skins BioAcceleration Technology employs a Lycra and Meryl microfiber fabric that has been engineered to form a gradient compression garment. The advantage of this functionally gradient system is that it can selectively apply compression to optimize bloodflow and the delivery of oxygen to the muscles. Additional functionality includes climate control, wicking and protection against the sun, offering UPF 50+. The garments are part of a growing move in the customization of sportswear. The company has conducted extensive sizing surveys among their market, which reflect the different body build dictated by muscle tone with each sport.

Compression suit, *Skins, Australia.* Sprinter Daniel Batman training in a Skins compression suit. The garments are specially designed to optimize the body's power, endurance and speed of recovery after training.

HERSELF installation, the first public experiment for the Catalytic Clothing project, which looks to use the surface of textiles to purify air. The joint research project, led by Helen Storey, is being undertaken by the University of Sheffield, the London College of Fashion, University of the Arts London, University of Ulster and the Tactility Factory.

FASHION

The lowest temperature ever recorded was -89°C (-128°F) in Vostok at the Russian Antarctic Research Station in 1983. The highest temperature on record is 57.8°C (136°F) in San Luis, Mexico in 1933. The average temperature is a more comfortable 15°C (59°F). Our most comfortable temperature (without clothing) is 27°C (80°F) and we use an estimated 70% of our energy in an effort to maintain that temperature. Our clothing does not in itself provide heat, but it does allow us to retain and maintain the heat that we need.

The Outlast's phase change material (PCM) has proven very versatile in terms of the form in which it is used and the range of applications and climates in which it can function. PCM has the ability to keep the wearer warm when it is cold and cool when it is warm, maintaining a comfortable body temperature. The fashion and leisure industry is using the material widely. Rukka is using Outlast as a liner on the inner jacket of their APR AirVision jacket. Here it is used in conjunction with their own AirVantage system, which allows the wearer to adjust the mid layer manually for more or less insulation. The outer layer of abrasion-resistant Cordura fabric is, unusually, knitted rather than woven. This is to allow further air circulation without a loss of protection. Treré S.r.l. Hosiery Innovation has developed a Reactor range which includes X-Bionic. This is designed to allow the wearer maximum movement while insulating the body against cold and uses a material called Xitanit, which offers perspiration management while reflecting the body's own heat and insulating the body against cold and heat in order to maintain a comfortable temperature. A different solution is used by the WarmX brand. They have developed a range of heatable undergarments powered by a small mini-controller device slipped into a side pocket. A silver-coated polyamide yarn is used to conduct the current and heat the garment in selected areas. The use of a silvered yarn has the added benefit of being anti-microbial.

Just as the human body needs to be protected from extreme cold, another set of dangers are presented by exposure to the sun. There are several different kinds of radiation coming from the sun: visible (light), infrared (heat) and invisible (ultra violet) radiation, which is present but difficult to detect by temperature or visually. Although ozone in the atmosphere absorbs much of this cancer-causing ultra violet radiation (UVR) before it reaches our skin, it is absorbing less and less as it is depleted owing to human emissions. Although clothing in itself offers varying degrees of protection, as it literally forms a barrier between the wearer and the sun, there has been a marked increase in the development of clothing that is UV protective. Australia has the highest rate of skin cancer in the world so it is not surprising that much of the product development has taken place there. Not since the introduction of Lycra in the 1970s has there been such an impact on swimwear and summer leisure clothing design. UV protection in swimwear has become ubiquitous in Australia. Those exposed to the sun over long periods during the summer, such as children and surfers, often wear a long-sleeved UV-protective T-shirt over their swimsuit for added protection.

The consumer is often presented with a straight choice in clothing between natural and synthetic. We are now starting to see the two come together at every level from fiber and fabric construction to garment design. Motorcycle clothing is a good example of this, where shops present racks of leather or fabric (Cordura, aramids and some carbon fiber) based clothing with little integration between the two. This is starting to change as consumers demand the comfort and handle of leather with some of the abrasion resistance and added performance characteristics that technical textiles and their associated processes can bring. This has an additional advantage of allowing manufacturers to use a finer grade of leather, such as the Kangaroo leather used in Dainese's Tattoo suit. The main portion of the suit boasts a dramatic tattoo designed by the Australian tattoo artist Luca Ionesco. It is constructed using Dainese's own D-Tec process. The leather forms the base fabric, then a sandwich-type laser treatment is applied between it and the outer layer of Lorica artificial leather, normally used on racing boots. The laser working process has also been applied to the aerodynamic hump just below the neck on the back of the jacket. Where movement and flexibility are needed, such as the elbows, chest, arms and around the kidneys, bi-axial elastic inserts are used: single pieces of leather, elasticized by bellows, stretch the material in two directions to give the rider a greater ease of movement. This shows a marked shift in design thinking and consumer expectation. Although this is a limited edition piece, it does pave the way to future design in this area.

The line to be drawn between clothing that offers safety, protection, wellness or health is often a fine one. It is one often crossed by designers and manufacturers with good reason and innovative results.

Micro'be' is a collaborative project between Australian artist Donna Franklin and Gary Cass, a scientific technician based at the Faculty of Natural and Agricultural Sciences at The University of Western Australia. They are using biotechnology to look at how fabrics and whole garments might be produced in a more sustainable way in the future. Instead of using weave or knit, the garment is fermented using living microbes. The living part of Micro'be' is a colony of safe, non-hazardous micro organisms. The bacteria convert the red wine alcohol into vinegar with a cellulose by-product. It smells like red wine and feels like sludge when wet, but the cotton-like cellulose dress fits as snugly as a second skin. Experiments with Guinness produced the Guinness Dress first shown at the *TechnoThreads* exhibition at the Science Gallery, Trinity College Dublin. Though it is possible to produce a garment using the stout, the additional malt and extra sugars meant the bacteria struggled with the conversion to cellulose. The finished garment had a high sheen but retained a sticky rather than dry finish.

Our idea of what constitutes comfort, wellbeing and health differs dramatically from generation to generation. The narrator in Brendan Behan's 1953 short story, *The Confirmation Suit*, recalls how 'My grandmother took a bath every year, whether she was dirty or not'. Emerging technologies such as nanotechnology and biotechnology will open new possibilities for future generations. This is already raising questions about what it means to be human and the creation of the enhanced human, or cyborg. In response to this dilemma, the French

Bio-Suit, *Dava Newman, MIT/Dainese, USA, 2008.* Prototype silver Bio-Suit for astronauts. Combining expertise from the motorcycle industry with space technology, the garment is designed to offer improved comfort and mobility for the wearer.

Harlequin Coat, *Orlan, France, 2007.* Detail of biotechnological coat incorporating the artist's skin cells, a black woman's cells and marsupial cells in a coloured life-size mantle with diamond-shaped patterns to symbolize cross-breeding. It was produced at SymbioticA in Australia.

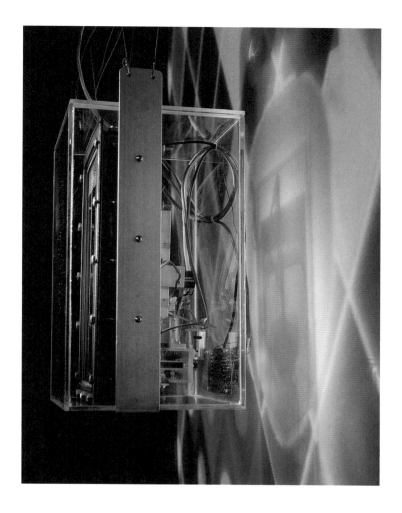

artist Orlan has created a composite biotechnological Harlequin Coat. For the artist, the harlequin conveys 'the idea of multiculturalism and the acceptance of other within oneself'.

As with much of her work, Orlan uses her body as the primary material. She has used her own skin cells as well as cells from a twelve-week old foetus of African-American origin and fibroblast muscle cells from a fat-tailed dunnart (marsupial). The in-vitro skin cells are placed in petri dishes then embedded in a life-size perspex coat with a diamond-shaped coloured harlequin pattern. The tissue culture bioreactor, representing the head, has been custom made and allows for cell growth. The coat is back-lit by a projection that shows time-lapse cell film. As the artist herself puts it, with the Harlequin Coat 'biotechnology is being taken out of the laboratory and turned into spectacle'. As this artwork makes visible to the naked eye that which is usually only apparent under a microscope, so the future impact of advanced textiles and technologies on the human body may become far more aesthetically and technologically explicit.

ENVIRONMENT

Palm Jumeirah, *Nakheel, Dubai.*
The artificial island measures almost
four square miles and is designed
to accommodate a population of
183,000. Geosynthetics are used to
provide 5,500 sq m (59,000 sq ft) of
drainage beneath the landscaping.

As human beings we have proven to be poor custodians of the world
in which we live. The onset of global warming, depletion of our natural
resources and the creation of toxic no-go areas have all taken their
toll. Compare our industrial production with that of the industrious ant.
Over millions of years the ant has generally succeeded in nourishing
plants, animals and the soil, but our manufacturing industry has been
in operation for a fraction of that time and yet has managed to wreak
havoc on just about every ecosystem on the planet. Now we have to set
about the task of putting it right.

There are currently myriad initiatives at local and global levels that
are trying to redress the balance. These include political, strategic,
social and design strategies; none is perfect but most are well intentioned.
This chapter will look at the way in which advanced textiles are helping
to repair some of the damage to the environment. We will consider the use
of advanced materials in areas such as the protection of plants against
the sun, soil- and rock-reinforcement, living roofs for buildings and the
use of advanced materials for alternative energy systems.

Rodsand Wind Park I, E.ON, Denmark. The company defines the challenges faced in offshore wind farms as WWW: weather, wind and waves.

ENERGY

Wind power is a growing alternative to fossil and nuclear power. Manufacturing cost is a driving issue in wind power and manufacturers are striving to produce composites in a more efficient and less labour-intensive way. Some new technologies are offering the possibility of savings on both material and manpower costs. The American company MAG Industrial Automation Systems has developed two pieces of equipment that have great potential in the aerospace and windpower industries. The first is the rapid material placement system (RMPS), which can be used for large-scale composites. It is a CNC automated cell that uses a rail-mounted floor gantry. Multi-axis end effectors can disperse or lay up woven or unidirectional glass or carbon fiber reinforcements and spray in-mould coatings as well as applying adhesives. The company estimates that two of these systems used alongside one another could each produce a 45-m (148-ft) blade shell in under two hours. A further development from MAG is the 5-axis gantry multi-processing system, which is seen as a companion to the RMPS. It can provide an unlimited x-axis range with an automated tool change and five controllable axes. It is specially designed for five-sided part access with additional manufacturing capabilities including cutting tools, spray heads, water-jet cutters, chopper guns and finishing tools. The machine is designed to reduce the time taken to apply coatings, blade machining and finishing, and the labour involved in these processes.

The Spanish company MTorres and wind-turbine manufacturer Gamesa Corporation are developing the concept of a gantry-based blade production process as the basis for a fully automated blade production system. Lamination is used in this instance as part of a structural process that is expected to see woven or dry unidirectional strips sprayed with an adhesive so that the fibers stay in position before being vacuum-bagged,

***Da Ban Cheng Wind Farm**, LM Glasfiber, China*. Rotors and blades are being hoisted at the wind farm, which has 200 turbines with a total capacity of 100MV and is located in the Xinjiang Province. The turbine is manufactured by Goldwind using LM Glasfiber technology.

resin-infused and finally cured. The gantry system is expected to have a lamination head connected to a vertical column that can move along the gantry crossbeam as the gantry moves along the full length of the blade skin mould. Six axes of motion within the lamination head will offer highly accurate placement of the strips according to a predetermined trajectory.

Kevlar mechanical paper can be used as a core component in the composite for the wind-turbine blades. A paper honeycomb core structure comprises sheets of high-strength Kevlar paper and bonding resin. The paper is sliced, glued and then formed into a series of hexagonal cells before being immersed in a bonding resin. The finished product looks like a cross-section of honeycomb; even the colour is a yellow-orange not unlike the colour of honey. The open space is over 90% of the area, so that the structural strength-to-weight ratio is excellent. The use of the lightweight, but mechanically strong material helps to minimize the rotational weight of the structure and increase the efficiency of the energy transfer in the wind turbine.

One of the most serious hazards that wind-turbine blades can face during their lifespan are lightning strikes. They can cause damage that is visible on the surface of the blade such as delamination and cracking, as well as hidden damage to the structure that will considerably reduce the lifespan of the blade. LM Glasfiber, based in Denmark, have developed a conductive system to combat this problem. The blades are fitted with lightning receptors that are specially designed to attract the strike to

Rotor blade testing, *LM Glasfiber*. The world's largest test bed for rotor blades is located at LM Glasfiber's factory in Lunderskov, Denmark. It can test blades up to 80 m (262 ft) in length using state-of-the-art testing methods.

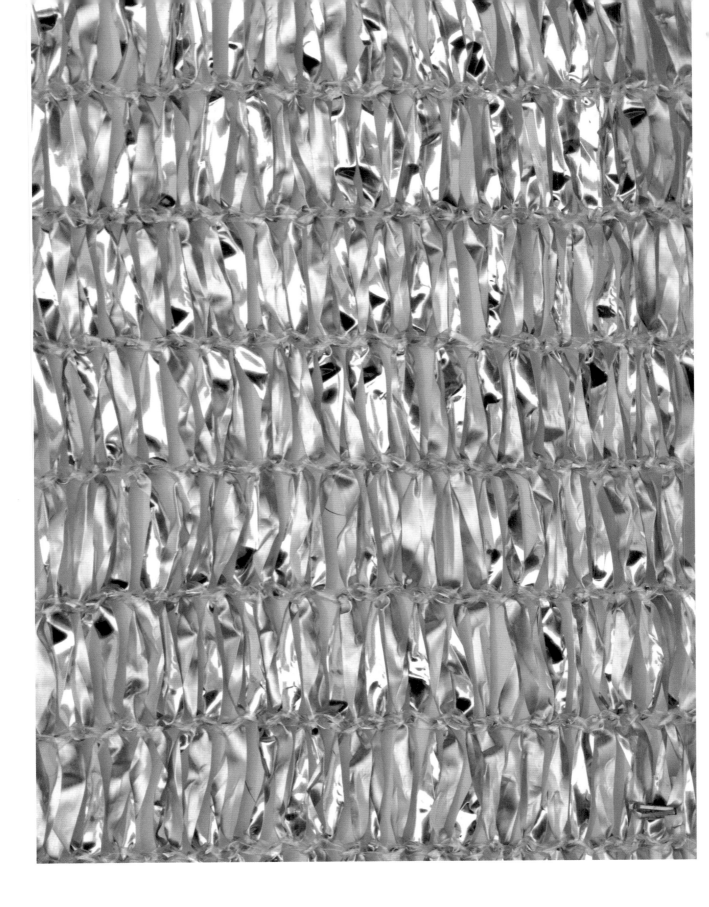

Opposite: ***Black shade cloth,*** *Genplus Corporation.* Hortisynthetic knitted tape polyethylene fabric used for plants to encourage growth in environments where sunlight is limited.

Left: ***Agrotkanina,*** *Wigolen S.A.* A range of polypropylene woven fabrics for protection against the sun, which also block the growth of weeds and reduce the need for herbicides.

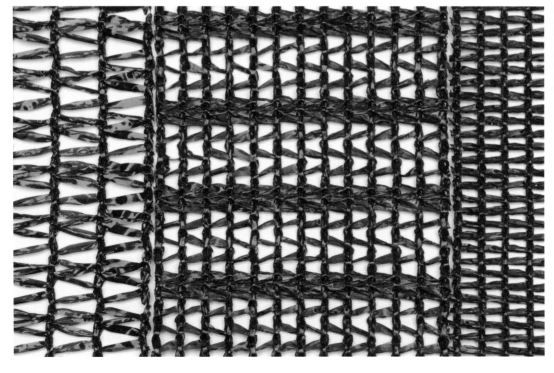

Aluminet, *Green-Tek.* Aluminet 'Cool Shade' UV protective aluminized flat tape cloth for plant protection offers the maximum amount of radiation reflection on both sides to reduce the heat inside as much as possible.

*Engineered Rock Placement Area
(ERPA), Cetco Contracting Services,
Pennsylvania DOT's Interstate-99.*
Geosynthetics used Texgrid from
Huesker, Geoweb from Presto
Geosystems and Geotex from
Propex Geosystems. Combined,
they offer containment, drainage
and reinforcement.

a particular portion of the blade where it will cause least damage. The
system uses a network of cables to lead the lightning current away from
the blade to the ground or to the wind turbine's tower. The receptors are
composed of a tungsten alloy that is conductive and offers high heat
resistance. This allows them to withstand several strikes and the design
itself allows this element alone to be replaced rather than the whole blade.

SOLAR PROTECTION

While the Maya and other early civilizations worshipped the sun, our
adoration today is more tempered. Sunlight is necessary for plants to
grow, but as temperatures increase plants must also be protected against
the harsh heat of the sun. This has led to advances in hortisynthetics
and membranes for biomes.

Hortisynthetics are knitted and woven in structure and made of
polyethylene or polyester base fiber or flat tape designed to protect
young plants, in particular, against drying out in the heat. The American
manufacturer Green-Tek produce a number of protective fabrics that
offer shade along with good ventilation and water access to plants.
A standard black shade cloth is used to absorb the sun's heat on darker
days to encourage plant growth. The white knitted shade cloth is used
mainly for flowering plants. It is designed to absorb and reflect the white
scattered light from the environment. This leaves the plants cooler than
if they were covered by a black shade cloth.

Two Australian companies are using high-density polyethylene (HDPE) for shade cloth. Polyfab Australia is employing a knitted HDPE to provide sun protection for the oyster industry, where it is used on oyster trays, and Gale Pacific Ltd specialize in shade cloth in applications including agriculture, horticulture and housing. The synthesis range of HDPE knitted fabrics carries a ten-year UV warranty against rot and moisture absorption, essential in tropical climates. The UV stabilized HDPE monofilament and tapes are knitted using a lock-stitch process. Depending on the grade, it offers a sun block factor of up to 80%. Applications include weather and pest protection for plants as well as shade for livestock and vehicles.

Transparent membranes are predominantly used in architecture, but are now also being used instead of glass in biomes. They provide heat and light for the plants to grow, but the exposure is being tempered. In China the NanJing Design Institute of Architecture has designed an extensive biome for the Nantong Horticulture Exhibition Garden. The tensile dome uses inflated ETFE for its high level of transparency, strength and lightness. The weight is a fraction of the equivalent glass structure. Two hundred and fifty hexagonal and polygonal ETFE pillows are used. They are composed of three layers into which the air is pumped to inflate the structure.

The All England Lawn Tennis Club (AELTC) host the world's most famous tennis event each year at Wimbledon. Rain is a constant concern, often causing serious interruption to the schedule. Organizers have been reluctant to cover the grounds and lose the grass lawn, so they have installed a retractable roof to protect the surface during play but still allow the lawn to grow. The roof uses a transluscent Tenara fabric from W. L. Gore and Associates. The primary function is to keep the rain out but let in natural light. It also means that the grass will not suffer from being waterlogged, while at the other extreme it can be used to provide UV protection on very hot days. Structural engineers Capita Symonds have installed an air management system to keep humidity and moisture at a manageable level when the roof is closed during summer rains.

Hydrotex, *De Saedeleir*. The nonwoven combines a filter and a drainage layer which have been needled together to form a three-dimensional protective and reinforcement fabric.

LAND PROTECTION

Humans, animals, and environmental and climate conditions are taking their toll on the land and coastal areas of our planet. There are a range of advanced textiles, including geotextiles, geomembranes, geonets, geomeshes, geogrids and geomats, which are being used in this area. Polyester, polypropylene and biodegradable materials are being developed out of environmental considerations with an increasing trend towards bringing in additional capabilities both in the materials themselves and the systems utilizing them. Niche markets are often growing in direct proportion to increased innovation and refinement.

The blanket bogs on the slopes of the Cuilcagh Mountains in County Fermanagh, Ireland have been referred to as Ireland's own Amazon rainforest. Their ecological importance has been recognized by UNESCO, who awarded the area Global Geopark status in 2007. The bog is home to a variety of wildlife and also performs an important function, acting as a natural sponge for carbon dioxide. In addition it has an economic function, providing peat or turf for fuel and is also a tourist attraction. Both of these industries are having an impact on the natural environment, particularly the industrial harvesting of peat. Traditional hand-cutting of turf means that the top layer is lifted up carefully to preserve the lower layers, so protecting and helping to replenish the peat. In contrast, the mechanical process removes the top layers and exposes those underneath, causing problems with drainage and defoliation. The restoration process is twofold. The first has seen the restoration of the bogs themselves using dams made from predominantly natural materials such as straw and wood. The second procedure is aimed at maintaining this development by establishing a series of floating roads based on engineering principles from the road industry. A shallow trench is dug first, cleared of debris and then a geogrid is laid into it, forming the raft-like aggregate path.

Drefon used in water ponds housing artificial snow guns, Manifattura Fontana S.p.a., Switzerland. The needle-punched nonwoven is made using high tenacity fibers for high puncture resistance. The Matterhorn can be seen in the distance.

Geogrid. Woven geogrids offer reinforcement for soil and rocks. This one, with larger aperture structures, was designed for rock containment.

Just how interconnected our delicate ecosystem is can be seen when the introduction of one environmental benefit can lead to problems elsewhere. The Maple Ridge Wind Farm located in upstate New York generates around 240 megawatts of electricity, enough for the needs of around 60,000 residents. During construction, the access roads to the farm needed to be upgraded to withstand heavy traffic that included 800-ton cranes. A geogrid was installed on 26 miles of road as well as under the crane platforms. The effect was to stabilize the soil and reduce the amount of aggregate and associated cost needed to reinforce the roads. An intelligent geosynthetic application has been developed by SNCF, the French railway company, with the geosynthetic company TenCate. The GeoDetect system uses a geocomposite to fulfil both reinforcement and monitoring functions, and has been used on part of the Mouchard–Bourg railway line in France. The geocomposite is used along a 50-m (164-ft) length of track that has a history of damage due to underlying strata thought to contain large cavities. GeoDetect reinforces the soil structure and continues to monitor any structural changes to the ground using a series of sensors embedded in the geocomposite, which relay information to a designated computer. The system is an extension of the French Railways RAFAEL project undertaken in the late 1990s and has potential applications in other areas that have similar problems, such as roads, tunnels and underground structures.

The Tessman Road Landfill site in San Antonio, Texas, is home to a sustainable energy supply. Republic Services Inc. has installed a geomembrane system in their landfill sites that will utilize decomposing waste for energy production. This has been installed on a number of sites, but the San Antonio plant goes a stage further by harnessing solar power in addition to the biogas-to-energy recovery system. The core biogas-to-energy system collects and processes biogas produced naturally as waste decomposes. The solar power element is an addition to this core system, and the company plans to retrofit it on existing landfill sites that are near capacity. Flexible photovoltaic cells from United Solar Ovonic LLC are adhered to a geomembrane from Firestone Specialty Products, which is placed over the landfill as it reaches capacity, in effect acting as a lid. The site forms part of a sustainable energy park where the company estimates two fully operational systems will have the ability to create nine megawatts of power, enough to supply the energy needs of over 5,000 homes.

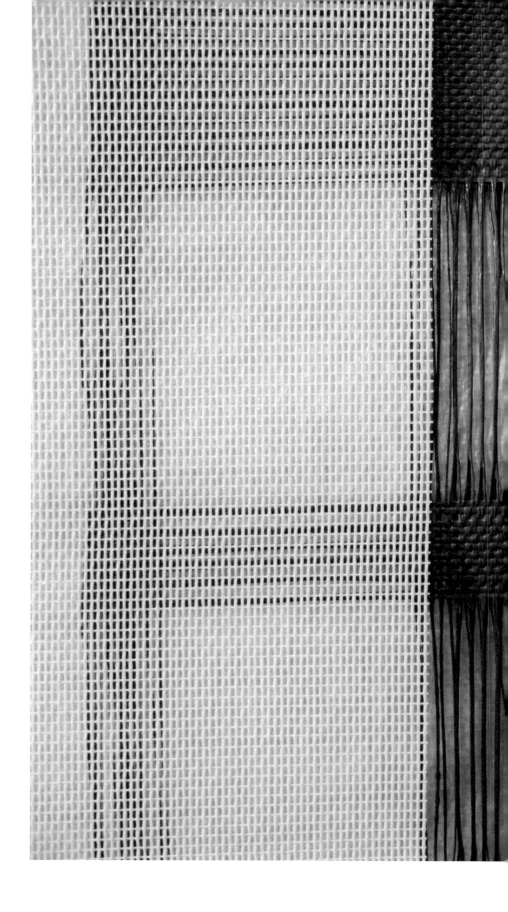

Geosynthetic. Using a sandwich structure to combine a geogrid for reinforcement and a tightly woven fabric for containment.

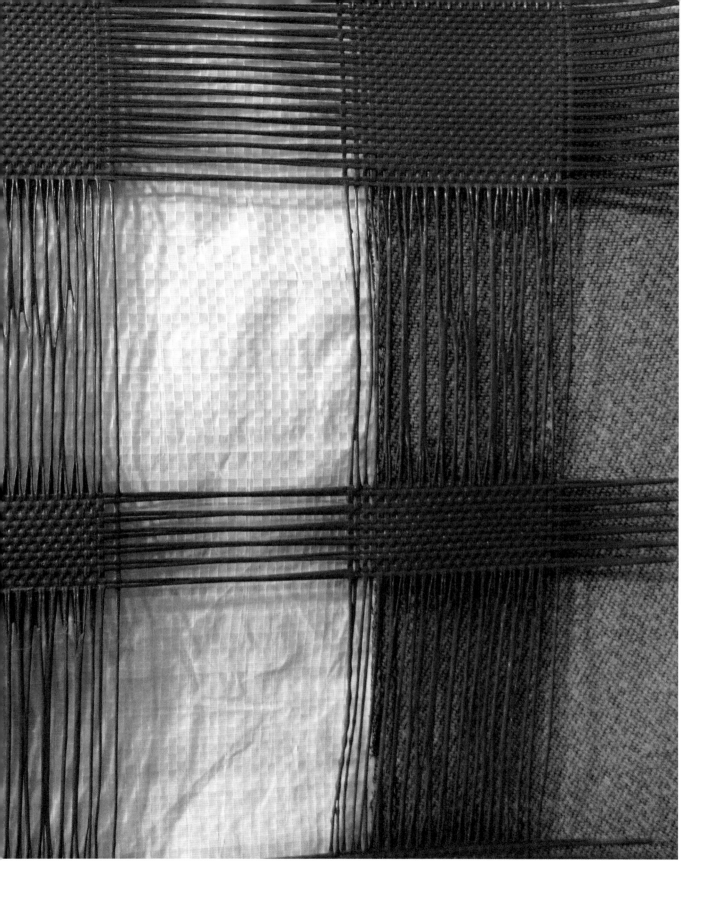

NENT landfill extension, *Hong Kong.* Tenax mono-oriented extruded HDPE geogrid has been used with a fire-resistant stone layer on the east slope where the geogrid is permanently exposed to disturbance by hillside fires.

Although the main function of geosynthetics is to protect land from erosion, they are also being used to create additional land mass. Hong Kong airport was built on an extended Chep Lap Kok. The area, previously home to a small fishing village, grew from two to seven square miles using geosynthetics as the basis for the development. The Palm Jumeirah development in Dubai is based on a man-made island of just under four square miles. Australian masterplanners PTW Architects provided for a population of 183,000 in their master plan for the development. Designed as an exclusive residential, hotel and leisure development, Atlantis is at the centre of the development and, as its name suggests, was designed as a pleasure palace of sunken aquatic chambers combining entertainment and luxury accommodation. The British company Environmental Sustainable Solutions Ltd (ESS) provided over 5,500m^2 (59,000 ft^2) of their Aquacell 25 Pluvial cube drainage cells to form a soakway beneath the landscaping. The system is modular so that a number of units can be stacked vertically as well as running horizontally along or just below the soil. The storm water management process allows for the filtration and reuse of water collected. AquaDrain geocomposite, another product by the company, is designed to help plants to grow on living roofs and to provide sub-surface drainage so that they do not get waterlogged. A welded Tuflex membrane forms the first waterproof layer. This is followed by a layer of Geo-tex 225 geotextile placed over cells and covered with about 5 mm (⅛in.) of sand. AquaDrain is then used to create a uniform drainage blanket before the soil mix and plants are placed.

Artificial turf for sporting events and children's play areas is a developing industry area. There is growing demand for geosynthetics that supplement or take the pressure off natural resources. Tessiture Pietro Radici S.p.a. is developing a number of products for this market. The yarns range from monofilament, which gives a very realistic appearance and is hard-wearing, to fibrillated polyethylene yarn and polypropylene yarns, which can be engineered to give textures a three-dimensional finish, so creating bulk. The majority are 100% synthetic,

Hurricane devastation, 2010.
Overflight by the US Coast Guard
to assess the damage caused by
Hurricane Earl to the shoreline
from Ocracoke Island to Elizabeth
City in North Carolina.

but there are now products that allow the artificial and natural to be
combined so that new grass can be encouraged to grow, with the artificial
acting to reinforce and protect. Desso has developed an artificial grass
that allows the natural grass to grow through it so that the synthetic
is supplementing the natural. The system has been used at Arsenal's
Emirates Stadium in London. In this, as in other sectors, man and nature
are coming together to help conserve the world that we live in.

COASTAL AND OCEAN PROTECTION

Coastal erosion is a worldwide and continuous problem. It is proving
a significant challenge to the geosynthetics industry because each
environment is unique both in terms of the soil and sand structure
and the causes and effects. Central American countries such as Mexico
are at the centre of the storm during hurricane season. The Yucatán
Peninsula has a dual economy of salt extraction and tourism.
Salt-producing sand dunes can produce up to 500,000 tons of salt
a year. Dunes connect the system of lagoons, but many of these were
destroyed by Hurricane Wilma in 2005, which had an impact on both
industries as well as being an environmental disaster. Geotextile tubes
have been used subsequently to reinforce the dunes around Coloradas.
They are covered with sand and planted with native coastal plants to
help protect against wind erosion and allow the area to start to recover
environmentally and economically.

Narrowneck Reef, *Elcorock,*
Queensland, Australia. Aerial view
of the artificial reef constructed
using geosynthetic Elcorock mega
containers. As well as reinforcement,
it performs an important function
in attracting sealife such as crinoid
and soft coral.

Elcomax in Clifton Springs, *Elcorock,* *Queensland, Australia.* A hard-wearing Elcomax nonwoven geosynthetic has been used in these reinforcement bags containing sand.

Tidal flats and marshland, *southern Louisiana, USA.* Coast Guard members and civilian boat crews are working to boom off inlets to these areas in order to prevent contamination of one of the Gulf Coast's most sensitive eco systems.

The Australian company Elcorock produce geotextile sand containers to combat coastal erosion and protect shorelines. The Elcorock container is based on Elcomax, a highly durable polyester/polypropylene needle-punched nonwoven geotextile which is UV-resistant and highly durable against turbulent coastal conditions. An overlock stitch is used on the seams to strengthen the construction further. The containers vary in scale from small bags which can be filled with sand and stacked along the sand bank, to the larger mega containers, which are made to order for applications that include reef, breakwater and bund structures. Because of the scale, they have to be filled hydraulically using dredges, sand or jet pumps. Elcorock mega containers have been used in the construction of Narrowneck Reef in Surfers Paradise, Queensland, one of the largest and most ambitious projects of its kind in the world. The reef measures 450 m (1,475 ft) in length and 250 m (820 ft) in width, requiring 400 containers that each measure 20 m (65 ft) in length filled with sand. A heavy grade of Elcomax has been used to prevent stress concentrations during installation and to withstand the heavy storms along the Australian coastline. The impact of such structures on marine life is also a consideration. Monitoring is continuous and within weeks seaweed was found growing on the containers, which helped to attract sea life to the area.

Geosynthetics are proving an invaluable material in the reinforcement of levees. In the aftermath of Hurricane Katrina, the US Army Corps of Engineers attributed much of the exceptional performance of certain levees, such as the St Charles and Jefferson, to their use of geosynthetics. The material is subsequently being used extensively in the restoration work in and around the city of New Orleans. More than twice the size of New York's Central Park, the Greater Grand Forks Greenway is a park area bordering the two cities of Grand Forks and East Grand Forks in Minneapolis. This was once the scene of a major environmental catastrophe in 1997 as flooding, and the fires triggered by it, caused billions of dollars' worth of damage. The 350-acre site acts as both a recreational area and a flood control zone for the cities.

Stone armouring was rejected in favour of a system that created a natural shoreline using native prairie plantings. A rigorous series of reinforcements lies beneath the greenery. Stepped plateaus have been built up with geosynthetic turf mats. Two different plant mixes were developed for the slopes, a shoreline and an upland mix. Both focus on robust plants that can thrive in difficult conditions. The shoreline mix includes big bluestem grass, milkweed, wild rye and local wildflowers. Located away from the river, the upland mix focuses on little bluestem grass with some black-eyed susans and prairie wildflowers. In 2001 there was another major flood in the area, but this time the levees held.

Our oceans are under increasing environmental pressure, whether from common waste such as non-degradable plastics or accidents causing pollution. On 21 April 2010 a fire on board the BP Transocean Deepwater Horizon drilling rig, 130 miles south-east of New Orleans, led to its sinking. This resulted in large-scale environmental devastation as the company struggled simultaneously to stop and clean up the subsequent oil spill. Hundreds of thousands of gallons of oil were spreading over the Gulf of Mexico daily. The geosynthetics industry offered solutions to some of the containment and clean-up problems with varying degrees of success largely because they had never witnessed a disaster of this kind on such a scale.

Deepwater Horizon disaster, Gulf of Mexico, 21 April 2010. Five US Coast Guard fire boat response crews battle the blazing BP off-shore oil rig.

Oil containment booms perform a primary role in forming a floating barrier to contain oil spills and protect the shore. Urethane and PVC form the bulk of the materials used. Cooley Specialty Products design fabrics specially for oil booms, which they often have to withstand harsh weather conditions alongside their containment role. The company use Coolthane thermoplastic urethane as well as Coolguard HRL Elvaloy. Coolthane is resistant to chemicals, UV radiation, abrasion and tears. The geomembrane uses heavyweight base fabrics that include ripstop and heavy denier yarns which are then coupled with a robust yet flexible polymer. The Coolguard (24 ounce) product is combined with DuPont's Elvaloy for high chemical resistance with a base ripstop fabric for tear resistance.

Hobbs Bonded Fibers manufacture a layered cotton and carbon nonwoven under the brand name Fibertec. It consists of two sheets of cotton with an activated carbon layer sandwiched in between. The material is designed to help in the clean-up of crude oil on beaches. It works to clean up the actual oil as well as absorbing polycyclic aromatic hydrocarbons (PAHs), thought to be a contributing factor to the toxic vapours that cause illness among clean-up crews. The material was originally developed to protect military personnel from chemical and biological warfare and is sold by First Line Technology, LLC.

LIVING ROOFS AND WALLS

Living roofs and walls is the term given to the growing of plants and grasses on the roof or walls of buildings. The Tyndall Center for Climate Change estimates that we need to introduce a 10% increase in urban green space to combat climate change. The benefits of these systems include a reduction in the urban heat island effect (UHIE), as well as improvements in biodiversity and acoustic and thermal insulation. The introduction of plants into or onto buildings has also been found to have a positive biophilic impact on inhabitants. Many of the textiles used in land reinforcement

Living rooftop of CH2, Fytowall, Melbourne, 2006. Located in the heart of the city, the building is a council workplace as well as being a flagship for the green workplace. The living roof is part of this philosophy.

are utilized here and some have been further developed for this specific application. Added functionality is also becoming more widespread as architects, engineers and landscape designers come together to harness some of the benefits generated by the system. As with the advent of architecture membranes, the living roof is changing the appearance as well as the energy performance of buildings. The natural and built environments are finally finding a way to live together.

The Ford Rouge Center in Dearborn, Michigan has undergone an extensive transformation that has seen the installation of the largest living roof in the world, measuring 42,000 sq m (454,000 sq ft). The masterplanning and storm water management plan was undertaken by architects and community design practice William McDonough + Partners. McDonough is co-author of the seminal book on sustainability, *Cradle to Cradle: Remaking the Way We Make Things* (2002), which includes references to the project. The membrane roof, complete with vegetation blanket of sedum, weighs under 15 pounds per square foot even when heavily soaked in rainwater. Because the membrane is protected from UV light and the thermal shock caused by hot days and cold nights, Ford expect the roof to last twice as long as it might otherwise. Manufacturing contaminants present in the soil are starting to be removed using an experimental process called phytoremediation. This new technique sees environmental problems addressed through the use of plants to mitigate the problem without the need to excavate and dispose of the contaminated earth elsewhere. The Canadian textile manufacturer Xero Flor produce the lightweight extensive

Ford Rouge Center, William McDonough + Partners, Dearborn, Michigan, 2003. Designed using the environmental principles outlined in McDonough and Braungart's book *Cradle to Cradle: Remaking the Way We Make Things* (2002), it includes a ten-acre living roof that also provides thermal and acoustic insulation for workers.

geomats used in the roof. They provide insulation as well as the basis for vegetation to grow with little irrigation. Since the installation of the roof wildlife has flourished, with regular sightings of Canada geese, mallard ducks and killdeer nesting and raising offspring.

The award-winning California Academy of Sciences in San Francisco is designed by architect Renzo Piano. Central to the design is a living roof. The geotextile used is biodegradable so that when the plants are strong enough to take hold the fabric will start to degrade. Alongside this, the architect has introduced a series of 60,000 photovoltaics to form the perimeter of the roof. These are expected to generate around 766,800MJ of energy annually, meeting about 10% of the building's electricity needs.

Malaysian architect Ken Yeang's bioclimatic skyscrapers first emerged in the 1990s. At a time when most of the high-rise structures were clad in glass, those designed by him stood out because of their lack of organic forms and the omnipresence of flora. The architect works on the premise that tall buildings should be treated like cities and as such should be planned in a similar way to include open green spaces. The Tokyo Nara Tower was groundbreaking when it was built in 1994. The 80-storey building uses a spiralling floor plan that climbs towards the sky with overhanging layers providing shelter and climate control for those below. It acts as a climatic filter, contributing towards better air quality, and noise and temperature control. Vegetation morphs with the building to create a modern-day Hanging Gardens of Babylon. Yeang has further refined and developed his approach to bioclimatic towers, but the Tokyo Nara Tower, with its robotic arms to care for the vegetation, is the structure that remains in the public consciousness as a vision of the future.

Workers installing the living roof, seen on the dome of the California Academy of Sciences, San Francisco.

California Academy of Sciences,
Renzo Piano, San Francisco. The
museum is situated in the heart of
the Golden Gate Park. Surrounded by
parkland, the building incorporates
a living roof so that it appears to fit
into a sleeve in the landscape.

Carpobrotus glaucescens, Patonga, Australia. The succulent has fleshy leaves and the bright pink flowers are in bloom most of the year. They grow readily in shallow and sandy soil, making them ideal for preventing coastal erosion and for use in living walls and roofs where soil conditions are equally challenging.

Australian Chris Johnson, in his role as New South Wales Government Architect, was responsible for overseeing much of the greening of Sydney. One of the projects on which his office worked was a reworking of part of the Conservatorium of Music, located in the heart of the city's Royal Botanic Gardens. While the original building dates from 1820, more recent additions from the 1960s needed to be improved in a way that would be more functional and less intrusive on the surrounding gardens. The architect decided to create an envelope by continuing the landscaping over the terrace and locating the new building below. As Johnson describes it in his book *Greening Cities: Landscaping the Urban Fabric*, 'The solution represents a new approach to a land-based green architecture that favours the overall landscape over the precious object'.

Market gardens are by no means a new phenomenon, but what is new is finding them on city rooftops. In some of America's largest cities, such as New York and San Francisco, residents are doing just that and starting small farms and market gardens on the roofs of their buildings. In Brooklyn, New York, Lisa Goode, founder of Goode Green, has started a farm on top of her building. Two hundred thousand pounds of soil have been crane lifted to the site and more than 30 crops, including lettuce, tomatoes and rainbow chard, are now thriving there. The response from local people has been tremendous. Restaurants are using the produce and a market has been set up so people can buy direct. There is also a strong volunteer force, made up in part by people who have been made redundant during the recession and are looking to discover

Vertical garden, Fytowall, Claude Sebastian, Sydney. This menswear store has integrated the vertical garden into their Martin Place store. Shelving holding stacks of shirts is housed within the vegetation.

The High Line, *Diller Scofidio + Renfro, New York, 2009.* The garden design along the disused railway attracted the involvement of the city community, giving a sense of ownership to the popular park area even before it was completed.

Chicago City Hall, *William McDonough + Partners.* Eleven storeys up, the $2.5m rooftop garden acts to filter out pollutants as well as regulate a reduction in the city's urban heat island effect (UHIE).

Proposal for an artificial roof garden, *Desso.* Artificial grass that allows natural grass to grow among it, effectively acting as a reinforcement for nature. Could this be the future, where the man-made acts to support nature?

a sense of community and individual identity. New York has a combined sewage overflow (CSO) to cope with excessive rainfall. When this system reaches capacity Goode claims that raw sewage is simply released untreated into the Hudson river. Green roofs can absorb a substantial amount of rainfall and, multiplied throughout a city, would certainly make a noticeable difference to the temperature as well. In an interview with the BBC, Goode put it simply, 'To get people really excited about something, especially when there is so much bad news out there, I think, is a really wonderful thing.'

The architecture practice of Diller Scofidio + Renfro is responsible for a 1.5-mile long public park that stretches from New York's Meatpacking District to the Hudson railyards in Manhattan. Built on an elevated railway, it effectively reclaims a region of postindustrial wasteland to give a portion of green nature back to the city dwellers of New York. The result remains in part architecture and in part parkland, providing a very different experience from Central Park just a few blocks away. Precast concrete opens to reveal wild grasses and then comes together to form areas of paving where visitors can congregate. ZinCo USA Inc. provided the green roof system of an egg-crate-type base that was then filled with gravel before being covered with a layer of TerraTex nonwoven filter fabric from Hanes Geo Components. Drainage is essential for this type of structure and it was wrapped with TerraTex, runoff water leading directly into the city's sewer system. Perforated metal layered with the filter nonwovens helps to hold the soil in place, while protecting against damage caused by rodents. In giving the area over to less formal planting, it leaves the visitor with a sense of discovery and an awareness of the changing seasons that a fully cultivated grass would not have given. The result is an urban version of the Burren region of Ireland, where plants emerge and find their own place amid an almost lunar terrain.

GLOSSARY

DIRECTORY OF SUPPLIERS

BIBLIOGRAPHY

PHOTOGRAPHIC CREDITS

INDEX

GLOSSARY

5-axis gantry multi-processing system: A CNC machine-tool platform that allows five-sided part access and is used to produce complex large-scale composites such as boat moulds and wind-turbine blades.

Aerogel: Produced by removing the liquid component of a silica, and other gels, and replacing it with a gas. The result is a highly insulating, but lightweight, material.

Alternative energy vehicle (AEV): A vehicle that runs on fuel other than traditional petrol or diesel, for instance, electricity. The term also includes hybrid vehicles, where one fuel source can be conventional.

Anti-bacterial: A coating or textile that inhibits the growth or spread of bacteria.

Aramid: Highly oriented organic polymer derived from polyamide with high density and low modulus, used where strength and stiffness are required in a fiber; examples include Kevlar and Nomex.

Biomimetics/biomimicry: Good design extracted from nature.

Biotechnology: Term given to any technological application that uses biological systems, living organisms, or their derivatives, to make or modify products or processes for specialist use.

Braiding: Weaving of fibers into a tubular shape.

Carbon fiber: Produced by the pyrolysis of organic precursor fibers, such as rayon, polyacrylonitrile (PAN) and pitch, in an inert environment.

Cellulose, cellulosic: Substance made from a natural source with many glucose molecules; examples include cotton and rayon.

Composite: Combination of two or more identifiable materials which have improved performance characteristics.

Ethylene tetrafluoroethylene (ETFE): A lightweight co-polymer originally developed for the space industry and now used as an architecture membrane for its weight, translucency and UV resistance.

Fiberglass: Filament made by drawing molten glass.

Filament: Continuous length of fiber. Silk is a continous filament, giving the fabric its beautiful drape and lustre. The fibers run parallel to each other, with no tangles or breaks in length. Most synthetics are made into continuous filaments to obtain smooth yarns.

Flocking: Fabric finish usually combined with printing whereby minute powdered fibers are fixed to the fabric surface using static electricity and glues.

Geogrid: Flat structure in continuous length or sheet form, mainly used for soil reinforcement and usually made from a polymer with straight or curved geometric aperture.

Geomat: Three-dimensional multi-layer structure predominantly used for the control of soil erosion and to provide vegetative cover.

Geomembranes: Can be made from a number of polymers with low permeability to provide a barrier to fluids.

High-density polyethylene (HDPE): A petroleum-based plastic is a polyethylene thermoplastic. The absence of branching means that it is a more closely packed structure with a higher density and chemical resistance than low-density polyethylene (LDPE).

Holographic: Effect achieved on foils, plastics, fabrics by applying a hologram, a photograph of a pattern (produced by interfering with a laser beam) that appears three dimensional under ordinary light.

Hortisynthetics: Knitted and woven fabrics used to protect plants against the heat of the sun.

Hydrophilic: Water-attracting. Molecules of a hydrophilic polymer attract water molecules and pass them along the polymer chain. Water molecules always travel from a high to a low temperature.

Hydrophobic: Water-repelling.

Knitting/knitted fabric: Fabric construction consisting of a chain of looped yarn, each row dependent on the last, made by hand or machine. Has a natural elastic quality and resilience. The vertical rows in a knitted fabric are the 'wale' and the horizontal rows are the 'course'.

Laminate: Two or more materials united with a bonding material, usually with heat pressure.

Living roof: A roof covered with vegetation to provide several environmental functions such as absorbing rainwater, providing thermal insulation and a habitat for wildlife.

Microfiber: Extremely fine yarns of one denier or less. As these fibers are so fine they can be specifically engineered to create a wide range of aesthetics and revolutionary performance characteristics.

Modulus: The measurement of a fiber or yarn's resistance to deformation.

Monofilament: Synthetic fiber made by extrusion process from a single polymer.

Needlepunch: Mechanical bonding widely used in the production of nonwovens. Needles are used to consolidate and entangle a loose web made of continuous filament or staple fiber to produce a stable bond.

Neoprene: Trade name for a synthetic rubber compound made from polychloroprene which is vulcanized with sulphur or metal oxide.

Nonwoven: Fabric with no formal structure such as weave, knit or braiding. Instead the yarn is laid in a loose web before being bonded by heat, adhesives, high-pressure jets of water, or needlepunching. With synthetics, heat and pressure are used to fuse the fibers. Nonwovens do not drape, stretch or fray and can be specifically engineered for different applications.

Phase change material (PCM): Capable of changing its state, for instance, from a solid to liquid or gas, in response to changes in its environment, usually temperature.

Photovoltaic cells (PV): A monocrystalline or polycrystalline silicone material that harnesses solar radiation and converts it into electricity.

Polyester: Thermoplastic fabric produced from the polymerization of ethylene glycol and dimethyl terephthalate or terephthalic acid.

Polyethylene: Group of semi-crystalline polymers mainly based on ethylene monomers. Polyethylene naphthalate (PEN) is a high modulus fiber.

Polymer: Material formed by the chemical combination of monomers with either the same or different chemical compositions. Plastics, rubbers and textile fibers are examples of high-molecular-weight polymers.

Polypropylene (PP): Semi-crystalline thermoplastic textile.

Polyurethane: Thermosetting resin prepared by the reaction of diisocyanates with polyols, polyamides, alkyd and polyether polymers.

Polyvinyl chloride (PVC): Polymerized from vinyl chloride monomers and compounded with plasticizers and other additives.

Rapid material placement system (RMPS): A quick cure mould-making system used mainly for the manufacture of large-scale composites such as wind-turbine blades.

Regenerated or 'natural chemical' yarn: Yarn derived from a natural source, such as wood pulp, chemically treated to create a new fiber. The first was viscose rayon and could be described as half natural and half synthetic. Different from pure synthetics, which are made from petrochemicals.

Resin: Solid, or pseudo-solid, organic material with the ability to flow when subjected to stress.

Resin transfer moulding (RTM): The process of placing a prepreg, fiber or fabric into a closed mould and then injecting resin into the mould and allowing it to 'cure' or harden under compression.

Sandwich construction: Composite made from a lightweight core material, such as honeycomb, foamed plastic, etc., to which two thin, dense, high strength or high stiffness skins are adhered.

Self-reinforced PET (srPET): Sustainable plastic composite composed from two fibers made from recycled PET bottles. Each has a different melting point, so that when they are woven the yarn with the lower melting point acts as a resin to bond the material.

Shape memory materials: These are materials, usually metals or polymers, that are said to 'remember' and return to their original form when subjected to heat.

Sheet mould compound or prepreg: Fibers or a fabric mat pre-impregnated with resin for further use in composite production.

Spun bonding: Continuous or staple monofilaments are spun to form a sheet before being subjected to heat-pressurized rollers, which weld the filaments together at their contact points.

Stitch bonding: Process of bonding together fibers (particularly multifilaments) by stitching.

Stretch: In a 'warp stretch', the elasticity runs parallel to the selvedge of a woven textile. A 'weft stretch' runs horizontally from selvedge to selvedge. A 'Bi-stretch' or 'two-way stretch' runs in both directions. A stretch fabric normally incorporates an elastic yarn such as Lycra. Cutting a woven fabric on the bias, or diagonal, also imparts stretch. Knitted fabrics have natural stretch due to their method of construction. Nonwovens do not stretch unless made from an elastic yarn.

Substrate: Background or base to which a finish or treatment is applied.

Thermal bonding: Process of heat-bonding in which the outer surface of filaments is melted, allowing crossover points to be fused together. Used for bonding polypropylene continuous filament.

Thermoplastic: Quality of a fiber whose molecular structure breaks down and becomes fluid at a certain temperature, making it possible to reshape the fabric by pleating, moulding, vacuum forming or crushing. The fabric is 'fixed' on cooling and cannot be altered unless heated to a temperature greater than the one at which it was reshaped. Most synthetics are thermoplastic and among natural textiles, wool possesses this characteristic.

Thermosetting polyester: Group of resins produced by dissolving unsaturated (generally linear) alkyd resins in a vinyl-type active monomer such as styrene.

Ultra violet (UV) degradation: Breakdown of fibers when exposed to sunlight.

Vacuum forming: Process in which plastic sheet film is heated to a liquid state and placed in a mould in a vacuum former; all air is removed so that the plastic takes on the shape of the mould. This becomes permanent on cooling. Used for subtle relief textures or dramatic three-dimensional forms.

Warp: Vertical threads fixed on the loom before weaving begins. A warp yarn needs to be strong and should not stretch.

Weaving/woven fabric: Textile structure made by interlacing warp threads with weft threads. The three primary weave structures are plain, twill and satin.

Weft: Horizontal threads in a woven fabric. Weft yarn can be softer and weaker than the warp.

DIRECTORY
OF SUPPLIERS

3M, USA
www.3m.com

AccuMED Innovative Technologies, USA
www.accumedtech.com
Aeronaut Automation Pty Ltd, Australia
www.aeronaut.org
Aquafil Textile Yarns S.p.a., Italy
www.aquafil.com
Architen Landrell Associates Limited, UK
www.architen.com
Arup, UK
www.arup.com
Asahi Kasei Fibers Corporation, Japan
www.asahi-kasei.co.jp/fibers/en/cubit/feature.html
Atlanta Nisseki CLAF Inc. (ANCI), Japan
www.clafusa.com
ATN GmbH Kreative Produktionen,
Germany
www.atn-vinyl.com

Bark Cloth Europe, Germany
www.barktex.com
Bayer MaterialScience, Germany
www.bayermaterialscience.com
Bekaert, Belgium
www.bekaert.com
Bell Helicopter, USA
www.bellhelicopter.com
Bill Burns, USA
www.safetygearforsmallanimals.com
BIOPRO Baden-Württemberg GmbH,
Germany
www.bio-pro.de
Birdair, USA
www.birdair.com
Blücher GmbH, Germany
www.bluecher.com
BMW, Germany
www.bmw.com
Boatspeed, Australia
www.boatspeed.com.au
Boeing, USA
www.boeing.com
Bruce Mau Design, Canada
www.brucemaudesign.com

Centexbel, Belgium
www.centexbel.be
**CIRFS (International Rayon and
Synthetic Fibres Committee),**
Belgium
www.cirfs.org
Clariant International Ltd, Switzerland
www.textiles.clariant.com
Cloud 9, Spain
www.e-cloud9.com
Cocona Inc., USA
www.coconafabrics.com
Concordia Textiles N.V., The Netherlands
www.concordiatextiles.com
**Cornell University, Textiles
Nanotechnology Laboratory,** USA
nanotextiles.human.cornell.edu

**CSIRO (Australian Commonwealth
Scientific and Research Organisation),**
Australia
www.csiro.au

Dainese, Italy
www.dainese.com
Daiwabo Co. Ltd, Japan
www.daiwabo.co.jp
Daly Genik Architects, USA
www.dalygenik.com
Design Composite GmbH, Austria
www.design-composite.com
Designskole, Denmark
www.dkds.dk
Desso, The Netherlands
www.desso.com
Diller, Scofidio + Renfro, USA
www.dsrny.com
Dimension-Polyant, Germany
www.dimension-polyant.com
Dow Corning, USA
www.dowcorning.com
Driessen + van Deijne,
The Netherlands
www.hildriessen.com
DSM Dyneema, The Netherlands
www.dyneema.com
Dublin City University (DCU),
Ireland
www.dcu.ie
DuPont, USA
www2.dupont.com

EDAG GmbH, Germany
www.edag.de
Elcorock, Australia
www.elcorock.com
Enric Ruiz-Geli, Spain
www.ruiz-geli.com
E.ON, Germany
www.eon.com
**ERG Materials and Aerospace
Corporation,** USA
www.ergaerospace.com

Fairey Industrial Ceramics Ltd, UK
www.faireyceramics.com
Formosa Taffeta Co. Ltd, Taiwan
www.ftc.com.tw
Formstark, Germany
www.formstark.com
Four Motors GmbH, Germany
www.fourmotors.com
**Fraunhofer Institute for Manufacturing
Technology and Advanced Materials
(IFAM),** Germany
www.ifam.fraunhofer.de
Fraunhofer IZM, Germany
www.izm.fraunhofer.de
Future-Shape GmbH, Germany
www.future-shape.com
Fytowall, Australia
www.fytowall.com

Gale Pacific Ltd, Australia
www.synthesisfabrics.com
Gamesa, Spain
www.gamesa.es
General Motors, USA
www.gm.com

Genomatica Inc., USA
www.genomatica.com
Genplus Corporation, Korea
www.genplus.en.ec21.com
Geofabrics Australasia Pty Ltd, Australia
www.geofabrics.com.au
Georgia Institute of Technology, USA
www.gatech.edu
gmp Architekten von Gerkan, Germany
www.gmp-architekten.de
**Gore Medical Fabrics
W. L. Gore & Associates GmbH,**
Germany
www.gore.de/medicalfabrics
Grado Zero Espace, Italy
www.gzespace.com
Green-tek, USA
www.green-tek.com

Hanes Geo Components, USA
www.hanesgeo.com
Hassan Group, Turkey
www.teksis.com
Helen Amy Murray, UK
www.helenamymurray.com
Helly Hansen, Norway
www.hellyhansen.com
Helen Storey Foundation, UK
www.helenstoreyfoundation.org
Hightex GmbH, Germany
www.hightexworld.com
Hobbs Bonded Fibers, USA
www.hobbsbondedfibers.com
Hollomet GmbH, Germany
www.hollomet.com
Huesker Synthetic GmbH, Germany
www.huesker.com

Innovatec, Spain
www.innovatecsc.com

John Deere, USA
www.deere.com
John Heathcoat Fabrics Ltd, UK
www.heathcoat.co.uk

Knippers Helbig Advanced Engineering,
Germany
www.knippershelbig.com
Kobleder GmbH & Co. KG, Austria
www.kobleder.at
Kvadrat A/S, Denmark
www.kvadrat.dk

Lenzi Egisto, Italy
www.lenzie.it
LM Glasfiber Group, Denmark
www.lmglasfiber.com
**London College of Fashion,
University of the Arts London,** UK
www.fashion.arts.ac.uk

Maccaferri, UK
www.maccaferri.com
MAG Renewable Energy, USA
www.mag-ias.com
Maharishi, UK
www.emaharishi.com
Manifattura Tessile Friulana S.r.l.,
Italy
www.mtfriulana.it

Marg und Partner, Germany
www.gmp-architekten.de
Massachusetts Institute
of Technology (MIT), USA
www.mit.edu
Methode Development Co.,
USA
www.methodedevelopment.com
Monsanto, USA
www.monsanto.com
MTorres, Spain
www.mtorres.es
Murphy Jahn Inc., USA
www.murphyjahn.com
Musto, UK
www.musto.com

Nakheel, United Arab Emirates
www.nakheel.com
Nanocyl, Belgium
www.nanocyl.com
NASA, USA
www.nasa.gov
Nike, USA
www.nike.com
Ningbo GuangYuan Fabric Co. Ltd,
China
www.new-fabric.com
Nuno, Japan
www.nuno.com

O'Neill, USA
www.oneill.com
Orlan, France
www.orlan.net

Palmhive Textiles, UK
www.palmhive.co.uk
PlanetSolar, France
www.planetsolar.org
Plastiki, USA
www.theplastiki.com
PTW Architects, Australia
www.ptw.com.au

Rebecca Earley, UK
www.beckyearley.com
Rinspeed, Switzerland
www.rinspeed.com
Ronan and Erwan Bouroullec, France
www.bouroullec.com
RWTH Aachen, Germany
www.rwth-aachen.de

Scabal, Belgium
www.scabal.com
Scaled Composites, USA
www.scaled.com
Schappe, France
www.schappe.com
Schoeller Spinning Group,
Switzerland
www.schoeller-wool.com
Schoeller Textiles AG, Switzerland
www.schoeller-textiles.com
Seretex, USA
www.seretex.com
Seymourpowell, UK
www.seymourpowell.com
ShadePlex, LLC, USA
www.shadeplex.com

Shandong Shenghao Fiberglass
Co. Ltd, China
sdyuxin.en.alibaba.com
Shri Ambica Polymer Private Ltd,
India
www.ambicapolymer.com
Skins, Australia
www.skins.net
Smartex S.r.l., Italy
www.smartex.it
Smartfiber AG, Germany
www.smartfiber.de
The Smith Family, Australia
www.thesmithfamily.com.au
Snohetta, Norway
www.snohetta.com
Speciality Fibers and Materials Ltd, UK
www.specialityfibres.com
Spraygrass, Australia
www.spraygrass.com.au
Strähle + Hess, Germany
www.straehle-hess.de
Studio Geenen, The Netherlands
www.studiogeenen.com
Swerea IVF, Sweden
www.swereaivf.se
Swisstulle UK Plc, UK
www.swisstulle.co.uk
Synteen, USA
www.synteen.com

The Tactility Factory, UK
www.tactilityfactory.com
Tajima GmbH, Germany
www.tajima.de
Technical Fabric Services (TFS)
Australia, Australia
www.tfsaustralia.com.au
Technical University of Denmark,
Denmark
www.dtu.dk
Teijin Ltd, Japan
www.teijin.co.jp
TenCate Protective Fabrics,
The Netherlands
www.tencate.com
Tessiture Pietro Radici S.p.a., Italy
www.tessitureradici.com
Tokujin Yoshioka Inc., Japan
www.tokujin.com
Toray Advanced Materials Korea Inc.,
Korea
www.torayamk.com
Transhield Inc., USA
www.transhield-usa.com

The University of New South Wales,
Australia
www.unsw.edu.au
University of Sheffield, UK
www.sheffield.ac.uk
University of Ulster, UK
www.ulster.ac.uk
University of Western Australia,
Australia
www.uwa.edu.au

Vector Foiltec, UK
www.vector-foiltec.com
Verosol, The Netherlands
www.verosol.com

Virgin Galactic, USA
www.virgingalactic.com
VivoMetrics Inc., USA
www.vivometrics.com
Volz Luftfilter GmbH + Co.,
Germany
www.volzfilters.com

The Warm Co. Ltd, USA
www.warmcompany.com
Warmx, Germany
www.warmx.de
Waxman Fibers, UK
www.flamacryl.com
Web Dynamics Ltd, UK
www.webdynamics.co.uk
Wigolen S.A., Poland
www.wigolen.com.pl
William McDonough + Partners, USA
www.mcdonoughpartners.com
Woolpower, Sweden
www.woolpower.se

Zaha Hadid Architects, UK
www.zaha-hadid.com
ZinCo USA Inc., USA
www.zinco-usa.com
ZSK, Germany
www.zsk.de
Zumro Inc., USA
www.zumro.com

BIBLIOGRAPHY

Albrecht, Wilhelm, Hilmar Fuchs and Walter Kittelmann, *Nonwoven Fabrics: Raw Materials, Manufacture, Applications, Characteristics, Testing Processes*, Chichester, 2006

Anand, S. C., and J. F. Kennedy, *Medical and Healthcare Textiles*, Cambridge, UK, 2010

Antonelli, Paola (ed.), *Safe: Design Takes on Risk*, New York, 2005

Beukers, Adriaan, and Ed van Hinte, *Flying Lightness: Promises for Structural Elegance*, Rotterdam, 2005

Beukers, Adriaan, and Ed van Hinte, *Lightness: The Inevitable Renaissance of Minimum Energy Structures*, Rotterdam, 1998

Blechman, Hardy, *DPM – Disruptive Pattern Material: An Encyclopedia of Camouflage*, New York, 2004 and London, 2005

Briggs-Goode, A., and Townsend, K. (eds), *Textile Design: Principles, Advances and Applications*, Cambridge, UK, 2011

Brownell, Blaine Erickson, *Transmaterial 2: A Catalog of Materials that Redefine our Physical Environment*, New York, 2008

Braddock Clarke, Sarah E., and Marie O'Mahony, *Techno Textiles 2: Revolutionary Fabrics for Fashion and Design*, London, 2008

Earth Pledge Foundation (ed.), *Future Fashion White Papers*, New York, 2008

Earth Pledge Foundation (ed.), *Green Roofs: Ecological Design and Construction*, New York, 2004

Gwilt, Alison, and Timo Rissanen (eds), *Shaping Sustainable Fashion: Changing the Way We Make and Use Clothes*, London, 2011

Horrocks, A. R., and S. C. Anand (eds), *Handbook of Technical Textiles*, Cambridge, UK, 2000

Jayaraman, S., P. Kiekens and A. M. Grancaric (eds), *Intelligent Textiles for Personal Protection and Safety*, Amsterdam and Washington, D.C., 2006

Lee, Suzanne, *Fashioning the Future: Tomorrow's Wardrobe*, London, 2007

McQuaid, Matilda, *Extreme Textiles: Designing for High Performance*, New York, 2005

Müssig, Jörg, and Christian Stevens (eds), *Industrial Application of Natural Fibres: Structure, Properties and Technical Applications*, Chichester, UK and Hoboken, NJ, 2010

Quinn, Bradley, *Textile Futures: Fashion, Design and Technology*, London, 2010

Sarsby, R. W., *Geosynthetics in Civil Engineering*, Cambridge, UK, 2006

Scott, R. A., *Textiles for Protection*, Cambridge, UK, 2005

Seymour, Sabine, *Fashionable Technology: The Intersection of Design, Fashion, Science, and Technology*, New York, 2009

Shishoo, R. (ed.), *Textile Advances in the Automotive Industry*, Cambridge, UK, 2008

Stattmann, Nicola, *Ultra Light - Super Strong: A New Generation of Design Materials*, Basel and Boston, Mass., 2003

Van Langenhove, L. (ed.), *Smart Textiles for Medicine and Healthcare: Materials, Systems and Applications*, Cambridge, UK, 2007

Watkins, Susan M., *Clothing: The Portable Environment* (2nd edition), Iowa, 1995

PHOTOGRAPHIC CREDITS

Numbers refer to pages on which illustrations appear
(a above; b below; l left; m middle; r right)

2, 5. Paul Pavlou; 8. NASA; 9. Nakheel; 10. Masaya Yoshimura;
12. Bill Burns; 14. Jason Maconochie /William McDonough +
Partners; 15. Rinspeed; 16, 17. Orlan; 18. Kyunhoon Kim;
22. Studio Geenen; 23–25. Paul Pavlou; 26. Marie O'Mahony;
27. Paul Pavlou; 29, 30. CIRFS/Bianca Wendt Studio; 32a. Bekaert;
32b. Grado Zero Espace; 33. Paul Pavlou; 34. Nuno; 35–37, 39.
Marie O'Mahony; 40, 41. CSIRO; 44, 45. Paul Pavlou; 47. Nuno;
48, 50. Paul Pavlou; 51. Marie O'Mahony; 52–57. Paul Pavlou;
58. Hassan Group; 59, 60. Marie O'Mahony; 61. Spraygrass,
Australia; 62–67. Paul Pavlou; 68, 69. Tokujin Yoshioka Inc.;
70. Paul Pavlou; 71. Marie O'Mahony; 72–77. Paul Pavlou;
78. Masaya Yoshimura; 82a. Paul Pavlou; 82b. Schoeller Textiles
AG; 83. Scabal; 84, 85. Marie O'Mahony; 86a. Paul Pavlou;
86m, 86b. Schoeller Textiles AG; 87. Marie O'Mahony;
88. Schoeller Textiles AG; 89, 91, 92, 94–97. Paul Pavlou;
98, 99. Aeronaut Automation Pty Ltd; 100–103. Paul Pavlou;
106. Birdair; 107. Tim Griffith Photographer; 108. Arup + Ben
Mcmillan; 110–11. Birdair; 112. Maarten Noordijk Photography;
114. Kvadrat; 117–21. The Tactility Factory; 122. image courtesy
Zaha Hadid Architects, copyright Luke Hayes; 123. Tim Griffith
Photographer; 124. Jens Sølvberg; 125. Peter Rejcek/NSF;
126, 128a. Marcus Bredt/gmp Architekten von Gerkan, Marg
und Partner; 128b, 129, 130. Birdair; 131a. Marcus Bredt/gmp
Architekten von Gerkan, Marg und Partner; 131b. Birdair;
132–33. images courtesy Zaha Hadid Architects, copyright
John Linden; 134–35. images courtesy Zaha Hadid Architects,
copyright Roland Halbe; 136. John E. Kroll; 137. Knippers Helbig
Advanced Engineering; 138. Armand Terruli; 140. Vector Foiltec;
142. Nic Lehoux Photographie Architecturale; 147. Boeing;
148a. Claire Brown/Virgin Galactic; 148b. Jim Koepnick;
149. Scaled Composites; 150l. Institut für Flugzeugbau,
University of Stuttgart; 150r. Swissetulle; 151. US Navy
photo by Mass Communication Specialist 2nd Class Andrew
Geraci; 153. Ford Motors GmbH; 154, 157. Boatspeed;
158. PlanetSolar; 160, 161. General Motors; 162. UNSW
solar racing team; 164, 165. BMW; 166. Schoeller AG;
167. Seymourpowell; 168–69. Marie O'Mahony; 170–73.
Rinspeed; 174, 175. BMW; 176. EDAG GmbH; 177a. Marie
O'Mahony; 177b. Plastiki; 180, 181. Bill Burns; 182. NASA;
183. Grado Zero Espace; 185. Douglas Sonders; 186. Centexbel,
Belgium; 187, 189a. DuPont; 189b. Helly Hansen; 190. Kyunghoon
Kim; 191a, 191b. Karen Fleming; 192. Nike; 194. RipCurl/Ted
Grambeau; 196. Marie O'Mahony; 197. Skins; 198. Jon Daughtry;
199. Dainese; 200, 201: Orlan; 204. Nakheel; 205. Ole
Christiansen/E.ON; 206, 207. LM Glasfiber; 208–209. Paul
Pavlou; 210. Archie Filshill*; 211. Paul Pavlou; 212. Gerhard
Puhringer/Manifattura Fontana S.p.a.*; 214, 216. Paul Pavlou;
218. Gary Ng*; 219. US Coast Guard photography by Aviation
Electronics Technician 2nd class Kyle Kappesser; 220a South
Pacific Aerials; 220b. Steve Smith National Marine Science
Centre, Australia; 221. Katrina Lawrence; 222, 223. US Coast
Guard; 224. Fytowall; 225. Jason Maconochie /William
McDonough + Partners; 226. California Academy of Sciences;
227. Tim Griffith Photographer; 228. Marie O'Mahony;
229.Fytowall; 230. Iwan Baan Photography; 231a. Roy
Feldman/William McDonough + Partners; 231b. Desso.

*Additional thanks to Diana Davis and Elizabeth Peggs at
the International Geosynthetics Society.

INDEX

acoustic 8, *8*, 10, 31, *54*, *58*, 75, 94, 110, 112–24, *112*, *115*, *118–19*, *122*, *123*, 124, 148, 155, 161, 166, *167*, 188, 224, *225*
activated carbon 94, 127, 224
aerogel *110*, 111, 141, 184
aerospace 7, 50, 56, *56*, 146–49, *147–49*, 155, 205
anti-inflammatory 34
anti-microbial 7, 33, 34, *36*, 39, 87, 99, 166
anti-radar *53*
anti-static 7, 32, *32*, 52, 58, 90, 166
aramid 25, 27, *27*, 28, 29, 31, 32, 34, 46, 70, 74, 99, *99*, 103, 124, 148, 152, 155–56, 199
artificial honeybee silk 39, *40*
automotive *8*, 56, 57, 58, *58*, 75, 79, 88, 90, 94, 152, *153*, *160–65*, *168*, 171, *171–75*, *176*

bamboo *36*, 37, 75, 136
BioBricks 41
biodegradable 57, *59*, 212, 216
biomimetics 38, *39*, *90*, *166*, 175
biotechnology 6, *9*, 33, 39–40, *40*, 79, *79*, 199, 201
breathability 50, *52*, 82, 90, 175

carbon fiber 22, *25*, 27, 28, 31, 37, *71*, 79, 98, 99, 103, 146, *148–49*, 151, *151*, 154–55, 187, 193, 199, 205, 224
carbon nanotubes 38, 46, 90, 151, 175
casein *see* milk protein
ceramic fiber 36, 125
ceramic foam *55*, 56
chemical resistance 7, 33, 75, 89, 188, 190, 224
coating 7, 31, 32–34, 46, 49, *49*, 67, 79, 82, *86*, 87–90, *88*, *90*, 94, *94–96*, 99, 130, 175
composites 7, 8, 46, 50, 58, 70–79, *70*, *71*, *72*, 82, 125, 135, *136*, 146–56, *153*, *157*, *175*, 176, *177*, 205–207, 215, 218
compression 193, 197, *197*
conductive 38, 46, 52, 56, *71*, 83, 84, 90, 93, 116, 187, 190, 193, 207, 210
cotton 33, 36, 37, 41, 46, 52, 59, *59*, *152*, 187, 199, 224

drainage control 67, *204*, *210–11*, 212, 231

electrospinning *see* spinning
embedding 7, 37, 82–83
embossing 58, *82*
embroidery *see* stitching
energy absorption 56, 89–90, *89*
ergonomic 50, 146, *167*, 181, 193
ethylene tetrafluoroethylene (ETFE) 107, 110–12, 123–24, *123*, 136, *136*, 137, *139–41*, 139, 140, 143, 211
expanded polytetrafluoroethylene (ePTFE) 93

filament winding 75
filter *54–55*, *57*, 90, 124, 127, 139, 156, 161, *211*, 226, 231, *231*
finishing 7, 31, 32–33, *33*, 41, 82, 90, 93, 94, *119*, 205

flame retardancy 7, 34, 45, *49*, 50, 52, 58, 87, 89, 90, *97*, *113*, 116, 177, 187, *187*
foam 50, *54–55*, 56, 94, 187, *187*, 193
functionally gradient 49, 50, *51*, 197, *197*

genetically modified organisms (GMO) 40–41, *41*
geogrid *see* geosynthetic
geomesh *see* geosynthetic
geosynthetic 5, *8*, 49, *59*, 60, 61, *62*, 65–67, 67, *94–95*, *204*, *210*, *214*, 215, *216*, 218, *218*, 219, 220, *221*, 222–23
glass fiber 22, *25*, 31, 38, 45, *49*, 57, 70, 75, 95, 111, 112, 127, *128–31*, 129, 135, 137, *137*, 146, 152–53, 177, 205, 211, 216

high strength 45, 46, 58, *95*, 103, 127, 146, 150, 152, 154, 207
high visibility 33, 52, *94*
hollow fiber 28, 192
hortisynthetics 49, 59, *59*, 210
hybrid 22, 31–33, *34*, 50, 57, 70, 150, 152, 181, 187
hydrophilic 58–59, 154, 192
hydrophobic 111, 192

implant *see* medical

knit 22, 37, 50–52, *50–53*, *89*, 119, 136, 175, 198–99, *209*, 210–11

laminate 67, 93–103, *94–103*, 141, 152, 155, 166, 199
lapis lazuli *84*
leather 87, 171, 199, *199*
lyocell 34

medical 7, 39, 50, *51*, 56–57, 82–84, *84*, *83*, 90, 93, 182, 188, 190, *191*, 192
membrane 90, *106*, 110–12, *110*, 123–24, *129–31*, 130, *135*, *137*, 139, *140*, 141, 150, 152, *156*, 196, 210–12, 215, 218, 224–25
memory metal *see* smart materials
mesh 50, *62*, *65*, 67, 95, 127, 212
metal 32–33, *32*, *34*, 49, 50, *54*, 56, 56, 58, *67*, 68, *68*, 69, 82, 83, 86, *88*, 89, 95, *97*, 124, 146, 152, 166, 187, 190, 193, 231
microfiber 28, 33, *82*
milk protein (casein) 36
morpho butterfly 38, *39*
multifilament 50

nanotechnology 32–33, 34, 37, 38, *39*, *40*, 46, 82, *88*, 90, *90*, 199
natural fiber-reinforced plastics (NFRP) 152
nautical 193
nonwoven 28, 31, 36, *40*, 46, 57–60, *57–59*, 67, *67*, 68, 70, *82*, 90, 94, 112, 116, 154, *191*, *211*, *212*, *221*, 222, 231

odour absorption 7, *32*, *36*, 37, 50

perspiration absorption 28, 34, 50, 198
phase change material *see* smart materials
photovoltaic 33, 86, 141, 155, 156, *159*, *163*, 215
polyamide *30*, 87, 95
polyethylene 67, 103, 176, *209*, 210–11, 218

polylactic acid (PLA) 39
polymer 28, 49, 56, 79, *82*, 85, 86, 89, 94, 110, 135, 140, 224
polypropylene 49, 87, 152–53, *209*, 212, 218, 222
polytetrafluoroethylene (PTFE) *111*, 123, *128–31*, *136*, 137
print 58, 83–83, *84–86*, 110, 116, *124*, 139, 140, *143*

radio frequency identification (RFID) tags 84, 127, 129
recycling 58–59, 87, 94, 125, 152, *168–169*, 176–77, *177*
reflective 33, *85–87*, 150
reinforcement 66, *71*, 152, 154, 204–205, *210–11*, *214*, *216*, 220–21, 222, 223, *231*
ripstop 50, 224

sailcloth 98, *98–99*, 103, *102–103*
sandwich structure 66, 67, 68, *68*, 124, 155, 216
scent *32*
self-reinforced PET (srPET) 176–77, *177*
sensors 56, 83, 84, 86, 93, 129, 139, 147, 187, 188, 190, 215
shape memory alloy *see* smart materials
silicone rubber 89, *89*
silk 39, *40*, 46, *47*
sintering 56
smart materials 32, 46, 49, 56, 82, 83, *83*, 116, 117, 127–29, *166*, 193
solar 129–43, *128–43*, 155–56, *159*, *163*
space 5, *32*, 46, 82, 87, 124–25, *125*, 146, *148*, *167*, 177, 182–84, *182*, *183*, *185*
spacer fabric 50, *52–53*, *89*, 90, 175
spinning 29, 31, 39, *40*, 82
stitching 46, 57, 58, 67, 70, *70*, *71*, 135, 211, 222
stretchable circuit boards (SCB) 93
sustainability 7, 26, *26*, 31, 37, *37*, 39, 40, 79, 86, *119*, *136*, 139, 141, 146, 152, 154, *166–67*, *199*
synthetic life/biology 41

technonatural 34–37, *34*, *36*, 87
temperature 7, *7*, 26, 27, 34, 41, 46, 49, 50, *54–55*, *58*, 59, *59*, *67*, 82, *82*, 84, 87–89, *87*, 95, *99*, 106, 112, 124, 139, 171, 187, 188, *192*, 197, 226, 231
thermal insulation 67, 89, 95, 110–12, *110*, 116, 125, 141, 197, 224–26, *225*
thermoplastic 38, 56, 67, 75, 90, 93, 155–56, 224
three-dimensional fabric 46, 49, 50, *51*, *52–56*, 58, *66*, *72–78*, 70–79, 86

UV resistant 28, 37, 39, 49, 58–59, 89, 197

vibration 8, 56, 94, 146, 161
vulcanization 32

water repellency 28, 79, 83, 88, 90, *90*, 94, 95, 98, *136*, 175, 187, 193, 196, 218
weave 22, 34, 44–45, 46–49, *47*, *49*, *50*, 88, 103, 124, 187, 199
wicking 83, 193, 196–97
wool 32, *83*, 115, 116, 166, *168*, 171, *190*